T0375581

THE FIRST NOEL

CHRIST JESUS, THE NEW BORN ROYAL KING

BARBARA ANN MARY MACK

authorHOUSE®

AuthorHouse™
1663 Liberty Drive
Bloomington, IN 47403
www.authorhouse.com
Phone: 833-262-8899

Published by AuthorHouse 11/22/2024

ISBN: 979-8-8230-3870-6 (sc)
ISBN: 979-8-8230-3871-3 (hc)
ISBN: 979-8-8230-3869-0 (e)

Library of Congress Control Number: 2024925039

Print information available on the last page.

CONTENTS

ABOUT THE BOOK

THE FIRST NOEL CONSISTS OF GOD INSPIRED WRITINGS AND SAYINGS THAT ARE COMPOSED IN THE FORM OF POETRY. THIS FORM OF LITERARY WORK MAKES IT VERY EASY FOR THE READER TO FOLLOW AND COMPREHEND THE MESSAGES THAT ARE CONVEYED. THE BOOK PLACES EMPHASIS ON CHRIST JESUS AS BEING CHRISTIANS FIRST CELEBRATED CHRISTMAS. IT ALSO INCLUDES TWO SHORT BOOKS: TITLES ARE **I NEED YOU, O LORD GOD** AND **IN THE PEACEFUL TOMB WITH THE LIVING CHRIST JESUS**

ABOUT THE AUTHOR

BARBARA ANN MARY MACK IS THE GOD INSPIRED AUTHOR OF OVER 7000 BIBLICAL TYPE BOOKS, OF WHICH ARE MOSTLY INCLUDED WITHIN HER SIXTY-FIVE PUBLISHED BOOKS AND A MISSIONARY MINISTER. BARBARA WAS BORN AND RAISED IN THE STATE OF PENNSYLVANIA. SHE IS ONE OF ELEVEN SIBLINGS. BARBARA HAS ONE DAUGHTER (LA TOYA ANN ROSE ROBINSON) AND ONE GRANDDAUGHTER (AMYA PENNY ANYSIA TURPIN

DEDICATION

TO ALMIGHTY GOD AND MELANIE LEAR

ACKNOWLEDGMENT

AS A TRUE WITNESS AND BELIEVER IN DIVINE CREATION, I WILL SHARE SOME OF MY GOD INSPIRED WRITINGS AND BELIEFS WITH THE PUBLIC. FOR, I AM NOT ASHAMED TO PROFESS MY UNDERSTANDING OF THE EXISTENCE OF ALMIGHTY GOD, THE FATHER, ALMIGHTY GOD, THE SON, AND ALMIGHTY GOD, THE HOLY SPIRIT.

BOOK # ONE

THE FIRST NOEL

INTRODUCTION

CHRIST JESUS, THE NEWLY BORN **ROYAL KING-**
WAS SENT TO US BY ALMIGHTY GOD, THE FATHER,
TO DO A GLORIOUS **EARTH SHAKING THING.**

FOR, CHRIST **JESUS, YOU SEE-**
WAS THE FIRST **NOEL/CHRISTMAS** THAT
ENLIGHTENED EARTH'S NEEDY **RESIDENTS AND ME.**

FOR, HE, **THE FIRST LIVING NOEL-**
WAS SENT TO DWELL WITH US, AS HE SHARED THE
GREAT AND HOLY STORY THAT GOD, HIS HEAVENLY
FATHER, **WANTED HIM TO TELL.**

FOR, THE DIVINE **STORY, YOU SEE-**
REVEALED BABY JESUS' POSITION AS **A**
DESCENDENT OF DIVINE ROYALTY.

HOLY, HOLY, HOLY-
IS THE DIVINE POSITION OF CHRIST JESUS, THE FIRST
LIVING ROYAL NOEL, ALMIGHTY!!!

HOLY, HOLY, HOLY-
IS THE UNFORGETABLE POSITION OF THE NEW BORN
KING; THE ROYAL GOD ALMIGHTY!!!

3

PASSAGE ONE

INTO THE PEACEFUL NIGHT, CHRIST JESUS, OUR FIRST NOEL/CHRISTMAS GRACED THE WORLD WITH HIS HOLY PRESENCE, POWER, AND MIGHT.

CHRIST JESUS, THE FIRST NOEL/CHRISTMAS, SPEAKING TO GOD, HIS HEAVENLY ORIGIN AND FATHER

YOU HAVE SENT ME AGAIN, **DEAR HEAVENLY FATHER-**
TO SHARE YOUR DIVINE KNOWLEDGE TODAY, WITH YOUR **EARTHLY SON AND DAUGHTER.**

YOU HAVE **SENT ROYAL ME-**
TO ENLIGHTEN THOSE WHO WILL DWELL IN YOUR LAND OF THE LIVING **THROUGHOUT SWEET ETERNITY.**

DEAR FATHER-
OH HEAVEN AND **EARTH'S DIVINE CREATOR-**

YOU HAVE REVEALED **YOUR HOLY PLANS TO ME-**
SO THAT I CAN SHARE THEM WITH BARBARA, THE DIVINE **MESSENGER OF THE FATHER, ALMIGHTY.**

I HAVE **RETURNED, DEAR FATHER-**

Barbara Ann Mary Mack

SO THAT THROUGH BARBARA, I MAY MEET AND GREET **MY TRUSTING SON AND DAUGHTER.**

FOR THROUGH **THE YEARS-**
MY HOLY SPIRIT HAS VISITED **THEIR MANY FALLEN TEARS.**

I WILL AGAIN, BY **YOUR HOLY APPROVAL, YOU SEE-**
WALK THE LAND WHERE MY EARTHLY LOVED ONES DEPEND ON **THE HELP OF GOD ALMIGHTY.**

I WILL **WALK THE LAND-**
THAT IS APPROVED AND GOVERNED BY **THE POWER OF YOUR HOLY HAND.**

FOR, **HOLY AND TRUE-**
IS THE HEAVENLY LOVE **CALLED ETERNAL YOU.**

I WILL AGAIN, **DEAR FATHER-**
SPEAK TO YOUR WORTHY **EARTHLY SON AND DAUGHTER.**

FOR, **THEY TRULY-**
DESIRE TO COMMUNE WITH THE HOLY SPIRIT OF GOD, **OUR LIVING FATHER, ALMIGHTY.**

HOLY, HOLY, HOLY-

IS THE REALM OF HEAVEN SENT LOVE CALLED GOD, THE FATHER, ALMIGHTY!!!

IN THE HOMES OF **THE SPIRITUALLY NEEDY ONES-** I WILL VISIT YOUR EXCITED **DAUGHTERS AND SONS.**

FOR, I **AM, YOU SEE-** THE FIRST NOEL AND CHRISTMAS THAT **YOU ASSIGNED TO BLESSED ME.**

HOLY, HOLY, HOLY- IS THE HEAVEN DESCENDED CHRIST ALMIGHTY!!!

FOR, I **MOVE, YOU SEE-** IN THE MIDST OF **EARTH'S NEEDY.**

I HAVE RETURNED AS A NEW BORN **INFANT, YOU SEE-** SO THAT EARTH'S CURRENT RESIDENTS MAY GET A FULL TASTE OF **THE NEW BORN CHRIST JESUS, THE ALMIGHTY.**

FOR, ALTHOUGH I COME TO EARTH'S NEEDY LAND AS **A NEWLY BORN BABE-** I STILL HAVE THE DIVINE POWER AND AUTHORITY OF **THE GOD WHO DOES SAVE.**

FOR, HOLY AND **TRUE, DEAR FATHER-**

IS THE BABE THAT CAN SAVE HIS SINKING **SON AND DAUGHTER.**

HOLY, HOLY, HOLY-
IS THE NEW BORN BABE CALLED CHRIST ALMIGHTY!!!

LOOK **UPON ME-**
LOOK UPON THE NEWLY **BORN CHRIST ALMIGHTY.**

FOR, I HAVE BEEN **SENT, YOU SEE-**
TO CARRY OUT AND FULFILL **YOUR PROPHECY.**

FOR, YOU, **DEAR FATHER GOD-**
HAVE SENT ME AGAIN, SO THAT I MAY SHARE, AND MAKE KNOWN, **YOUR VERSION OF PERFECT DIVINE LOVE.**

CHRIST JESUS, OUR FIRST NOEL/CHRISTMAS, SPEAKING TO EARTH'S SPIRITUALLY NEEDY ONES

HOLY, HOLY, HOLY-
IS THE ASSIGNMENT THAT I HAVE RECEIVED FROM MY HEAVENLY GOD AND FATHER ALMIGHTY!!!

FOR, INTO **THE PEACEFUL NIGHT-**
I WILL RELEASE MY HEAVEN SENT **POWER AND MIGHT.**

FOR, I, THE FOREVER- **LIVING CHRIST JESUS-**
HAVE BEEN SENT TO HELP THE SINNERS AND **THE DIVINE RIGHTEOUS.**

FOR, **HOLY, YOU SEE-**
IS THE HEAVENLY ASSIGNMENT THAT WAS **GIVEN TO ME.**

HOLY, HOLY, HOLY-
ARE THE RIGHTEOUS LIVING CHILDREN OF GOD ALMIGHTY!!!

FOR, I COME TO YOU AS A NEW BORN **BABE, YOU SEE-**
SO THAT YOU MAY GET A TASTE OF **THE LIVING CHRIST ALMIGHTY.**

I AM PHYSICALLY ALIVE AGAIN, **THROUGH BARBARA-**
MY FAITHFUL FRIEND **AND DIVINE MESSENGER.**

I WILL TRAVEL WHEREVER SHE GOES, FOR I AM THE FAITHFUL ONE **AND DIVINE FATHER.**
AND, I NOW DWELL **MY OBEDIENT DAUGHTER.**

I AM ALIVE IN THE HOLY PRESENCE **OF ALMIGHTY GOD-**
FOR, I HAVE BEEN CALLED INTO HIS DIVINE EXISTENCE BY **THE POWER OF HIS LOVE.**

Barbara Ann Mary Mack

HOLY, HOLY, HOLY-
IS THE POWER OF GOD ALMIGHTY!!!

FOR, HE IS ALIVE AND FREE **THROUGH PERMANENT ME.**
HOLY, HOLY, HOLY IS THE REALM **CALLED GOD ALMIGHTY!!!**

I LIVE, YOU SEE-
IN THE MIDST OF THIS **WORLD'S TRAGEDY.**

HOLY, HOLY, HOLY-
IS THE NEW BORN BABE CALLED CHRIST JESUS, THE ALMIGHTY!!!

THE REALM OF TRUE UNENDING EXISTENCE HAS CALLED FORTH MY HOLY PRESENCE, SAYS THE LORD JESUS

<u>CHRIST JESUS, THE NEW BORN BABE, SPEAKING TO EARTH'S RESIDENTS TODAY</u>

I HAVE **RETURNED, YOU SEE-**
SO THAT I MAY COMFORT THE LOVED ONES WHO **BELONG TO ME.**

DEAR CHILDREN
YES! THOSE OF YOU FROM **EVERY BLESSED NATION.**

I AM HERE-
YOUR FIRST NOEL IS VERY NEAR.

LOOK AROUND, AND YOU WILL SEE-
THE GREAT AND HOLY WONDER THAT IS CALLED
THE LIVING CHRIST ALMIGHTY.

FOR, MY HEAVENLY RETURN, YOU SEE-
IS TO HAVE YOU ALL EXPERIENCE A TASTE OF
DIVINE REALITY.

FOR HOLY AND TRUE-
IS THE LORD AND GOD WHO WALKS IN THE MIDST OF
BLESSED YOU.

HOLY, HOLY, HOLY-
IS THE ROYAL GOD AND KING; CHRIST JESUS, THE
ALMIGHTY!!!

DEAR CHILDREN OF MINE-
YOUR HEAVENLY SAVIOR AND GOD IS WITH YOU AT
THIS PARTICULAR TIME.

FOR, YOUR HOLY GOD HAS JOINED, YOU SEE-
THE BLESSED ONES WHO BELONG TO ME.

REJOICE, DEAR ONE-

Barbara Ann Mary Mack

FOR, YOU ARE IN THE ROYAL PRESENCE OF GOD, THE
FATHER'S, **ONLY BEGOTTEN SON!**

I AM FAITHFUL **AND TRUE-**
AND, MY DEVOTION IS TO MY HEAVENLY FATHER
AND BELOVED YOU.

HOLY, HOLY, HOLY-
IS THE RETURN OF THE FIRST NOEL CALLED CHRIST
ALMIGHTY!!!

INTO THE SWEET, BUT **COLD NIGHT-**
I WILL KEEP YOU ALL WITHIN **MY HOLY SIGHT.**

FOR, HOLY, **ETERNAL, AND TRUE-**
IS THE HEAVEN SENT BABE WHO STILL **WATCHES**
OVER YOU.

HOLY, HOLY, HOLY-
IS THE DESCENDED BABE WHO WATCHES OVER YOU
AND ME.

FOR, DURING THE **PEACEFUL NIGHT-**
I, THE LORD JESUS, WILL SHINE **MY DIVINE ROYAL**
LIGHT.

FOR, **HOLY AND TRUE-**

IS THE BABE WHO HAS DESCENDED FROM SWEET HEAVEN, SO THE **HE MAY RESCUE.**

HOLY, HOLY, HOLY-
IS THE DESCENDED CHRIST JESUS, THE LIFE-SAVING GOD ALMIGHTY!!!

FOR, I, THE FIRST **CHRISTMAS, YOU SEE-**
HAVE BEEN SENT BY **GOD, THE FATHER, ALMIGHTY.**

I HAVE BEEN SENT, SO THAT I MAY REVEAL **THE HEAVENLY PEACE-**
THAT GOD, OUR **FATHER, DID RELEASE.**

FOR, **WE TRULY-**
LOVE THE GREATEST CREATION OF **GOD ALMIGHTY.**

I, YOUR LORD AND **SAVIOR, CHRIST JESUS-**
TODAY, WALK IN THE MIDST **OF MY RIGHTEOUS.**

FOR, THE **RIGHTEOUS ONE-**
WILL HAVE THE HONOR AND PRIVILEGE TO DINE WITH **GOD, THE FATHER'S, ONLY BEGOTTEN SON.**

FOR, **HOLY, YOU SEE-**
IS GOD, THE FATHER'S, ONLY BEGOTTEN SON, CALLED CHRIST JESUS; **THE HEAVEN SENT VICTORY.**

HOLY, HOLY, HOLY-
IS THE DESCENDED CHRIST JESUS; THE VICTORY.

HOLY, HOLY, HOLY-
IS THE FATHER'S VICTORY!!!

FOR, I HAVE BEEN VICTORIOUS OVER SATAN'S
REALM OF **EVIL AND DESTRUCTION-**
WHEN I SACRIFICED MY PHYSICAL LIFE, BY DYING OF
THE CROSS FOR **MY WORTHY EARTHLY CHILDREN.**

HOLY, HOLY, HOLY-
IS THE SACRIFICIAL ACT OF LOVE THAT WAS
PERFORMED BY THE FOREVER-
LIVING KING AND GOD ALMIGHTY!!!

I WILL MOVE IN THE MIDST OF **MY DAUGHTERS AND
SONS-**
AS BARBARA REVEALS MY HOLY PRESENCE TO
THE BLESSED ONES.

FOR, **HOLY AND TRUE-**
IS THE HEAVEN SENT SAVIOR AND GOD WHO NOW
MOVES IN THE MIDST OF YOU.

HOLY, HOLY, HOLY-
ARE THE MOVEMENTS OF CHRIST ALMIGHTY!!!

DURING THE CHILLY NIGHTS, **DEAR CHILDREN-**
MY HOLY SPIRIT WILL AWAKEN MY GREATEST
CREATION.

FOR, I WANT THE WORLD TO **SEE AND KNOW-**
THAT I AM WITH THEM **WHERE THEY GO.**

HOLY, HOLY, HOLY-
IS THE DESCENDED NEW BORN BABE CALLED CHRIST
JESUS, THE ALMIGHTY!!!

FOR, I **WALK, YOU SEE-**
IN THE MIDST OF THE CHILDREN WHO LOVES **GOD,**
THE FATHER, AND ME.

FOR, AS A NEW BORN **BABE, YOU SEE-**
GOD, THE FATHER, **TRUSTS OBEDIENT ME.**

FOR, HE SENT **ME TO DO-**
A MIGHTY WORK THAT WILL **HELP ALL OF YOU.**

HOLY, HOLY, HOLY-
IS THE DESCENDED BABE OF DIVINE LOVE CALLED
CHRIST ALMIGHTY!!!

<u>BARBARA SPEAKING TO EARTH'S CHILDREN TODAY</u>

I COME, **YOU SEE-**

WITH THE GIFT OF **DIVINE ROYALTY.**

FOR, CHRIST, THE FORETOLD **KING OF KINGS-**
HAS COME TO EARTH AGAIN, **WITH HEAVEN SENT THINGS.**

FOR, GOD, THE **FATHER, YOU SEE-**
HAS REVEALED HIS HEAVENLY PLAN TO **BABY JESUS AND ME.**

HOLY, HOLY, HOLY-
ARE THE HEAVEN SENT GOOD TIDINGS THAT WAS SENT TO US BY CHRIST ALMIGHTY!!!

HOLY AND TRUE-
ARE THE HEAVENLY GOOD TIDINGS THAT COME FROM GOD, THE FATHER ALMIGHTY, FOR ME AND YOU!!!

<u>**CHRIST JESUS, THE NEW BORN BABE, SPEAKING TO EARTH'S RESIDENTS TODAY**</u>

AS I WALK **EARTH'S BARREN LAND-**
I ENCOURAGE THE FATHER'S EARTHLY LOVED ONES TO TAKE HOLD OF **MY POWERFUL HAND.**

ALTHOUGH I AM A LITTLE **BABE, YOU SEE-**
I STILL HAVE THE POWER OF **GOD, THE ALMIGHTY.**

FOR, HOLY **AND TRUE-**
IS THE HEAVEN SENT BABY JESUS WHO HAS COME
AGAIN, TO **RESCUE SINKING YOU.**

HOLY, HOLY, HOLY-
IS THE LIFE-SAVING BABY, ALMIGHTY!!!

FOR, **BABY JESUS-**
HAS COME AGAIN, TO OFFER SALVATION TO THE
MEEK AND THE RIGHTEOUS.

HOLY, HOLY, HOLY-
IS THE LIFE-SAVING BABY JESUS; THE ALMIGHTY!!!

FOR, I **MOVE, YOU SEE-**
IN THE MIDST OF THE CHILDREN WHO **DESIRE TO
SEE ME.**

FOR, HOLY **AND TRUE-**
IS THE BABE WHO TRULY **ADORES BLESSED YOU.**

DEAR **CHILDREN-**
FROM **EVERY NATION.**

REACH **FOR ME-**
REACH FOR THE **DIVINE REALM OF REALITY.**

FOR, I AM VERY **NEAR, DEAR ONES-**

Barbara Ann Mary Mack

AND, I DESIRE TO MINGLE WITH MY EARTHLY **DAUGHTERS AND SONS.**

MY LITTLE CHILDREN-
TRUST IN ME, FOR I, THE LORD JESUS, **LOVE MY GREATEST CREATION.**

I ALSO LOOK **FORWARD TO-**
THE DAY WHEN YOU AND I WALK THE GOLDEN STREETS IN SWEET HEAVEN WITH **BLESSED SANCTIFIED YOU.**

I LOOK **FORWARD TO SEE-**
EVERY SAVED LITTLE ONE WHO BELONGS TO **THE FATHER AND ME.**

BARBARA SPEAKING TO EARTH'S SPIRITUAL NEEDY RESIDENTS TODAY

FOR **HOLY AND TRUE-**
IS THE GOD WHO WANTS **THE BEST FOR ALL OF YOU.**

HOLY, HOLY, HOLY-
ARE THE LITTLE ONES WHO BELONG TO CHRIST **JESUS, THE ALMIGHTY!!!**

FOR, WHEN I MOVE IN THE MIDST OF MY GREAT CREATION **THROUGH BARBARA-**

MY HOLY PRESENCE SHINES IN THE MIDST **OF MY OBEDIENT SON AND DAUGHTER.**

FOR, **HOLY, YOU SEE-**
IS THE FAITHFUL GOD WHO WALKS THE STREETS OF GOLD **IN THE MIDST OF ME.**

FOR, HOLY IS **THE BABE-**
WHO HAS COME TO **BACK TO SAVE.**

O FIRST NOEL

BARBARA SPEAKING TO BABY JESUS, OUR FIRST NOEL /CHRISTMAS

HALLOW, HALLOW, **HALLOW IS YOUR PERFECT NAME.**
HOLINESS, HOLINESS, HOLINESS IS YOUR **WORLD OF EVERLASTING FAME.**

FOR YOU, **O HOLY BABY-**
ARE THE ONLY BEGOTTEN SON OF **JEHOVAH GOD, THE FATHER, ALMIGHTY.**

YOU HAVE BEEN SENT TO US **AGAIN, YOU SEE-**
SO THAT YOU MAY OFFER SALVATION TO THE CHILDREN WHO **BELONG TO GOD ALMIGHTY.**

FOR, **HOLY AND TRUE-**

IS THE DIVINE HEAVENLY LOVE THAT WAS **SENT WITH YOU.**

HOLY, HOLY, HOLY-
IS THE FOREVER-LIVING BABE CALLED CHRIST JESUS, THE ALMIGHTY!!!

FOR YOU, O HOLY BABE AND **EVERLASTING FRIEND-** PROMISED TO STAY BY THE SIDE OF YOUR NEEDY LOVED ONES **UNTIL THE VERY END.**

FOR, **HOLY AND TRUE-**
IS THE HEAVENLY LOVE THAT DESCENDED FROM SWEET **HEAVEN WITH YOU.**

HOLY, HOLY, HOLY-
IS THE DESCENDED LOVE OF CHRIST ALMIGHTY!!!

FOR, CHRIST JESUS, THE **NEW BORN BABY-**
NOW WALKS IN THE MIDST OF THE EARTHLY **CHILDREN OF GOD ALMIGHTY!!!**

HOLY, HOLY, HOLY-
IS CHRIST JESUS' REALM OF EARTH AND HEAVENLY ROYALTY.

O FIRST **SANCTIFIED NOEL-**

YOU ARE THE HOLY STORY THAT I WILL **FOREVER SALUTE AND TELL.**

YOU ARE GOD, THE FATHER'S, **GREATEST GIFT TO US-**
FOR, YOU ARE OUR FIRST AND LAST **MERRY CHRISTMAS.**

YOU ARE **THE HOLY LOVE-**
THAT DESCENDED TO US FROM SWEET **ETERNAL HEAVEN ABOVE.**

YOU ARE OUR GREATEST GIFT FROM **SWEET HEAVEN ABOVE-**
FOR YOU, O BLESSED ONE, ARE GOD, OUR FATHER, GREATEST **GIFT OF DIVINE LOVE.**

FOR, **HOLY AND TRUE-**
IS THE FIRST CHRISTMAS GIFT **CALLED BLESSED YOU.**

HOLY, HOLY, HOLY-
IS THE ETERNAL NOEL ALMIGHTY!!!

MY BLESSED SOUL **MOVES, YOU SEE-**
IN THE MIDST OF **YOUR DIVINITY.**

FOR, YOU, **O LORD GOD-**

HAVE COME BACK TO SHARE YOUR **HEAVEN SENT DIVINE LOVE.**

HOLY, HOLY, HOLY-
IS THE FIRST NOEL ALMIGHTY!!!

HOLY AND TRUE-
IS THE GIFT OF EVERLASTING LIFE THAT **COMES FROM BELOVED, ROYAL YOU.**

MY BLESSED SOUL AND SPIRIT **REACH OUT TO YOU-**
AS I ENJOY THE HOLY PRESENCE OF THE KING AND GOD WHO IS **ETERNAL, LOVING AND TRUE.**

YOU ARE OURS; AND, IN YOU WE HAVE **PLACED OUR TRUST-**
FOR, YOU ARE THE ETERNAL GOD AND **FIRST CHRISTMAS-**

HOLY, HOLY, HOLY-
IS THE KING OF LIFE CALLED BABY JESUS, THE ALMIGHTY.

O HOLY BABY JESUS: I BOW IN YOUR **HOLY PRESENCE DAILY-**
FOR, I KNOW THAT YOU ARE **THE HEAVEN SENT ALMIGHTY.**

FOR, I TRULY ADORE-
THE HOLY FIRST CHRISTMAS WHO HAS OPENED FOR
ME HEAVEN'S WONDERFUL DOOR.

HOLY, HOLY, HOLY-
IS THE GREAT KING AND GOD; CHRIST JESUS, THE
ALMIGHTY!!!

FOR, HOLY AND TRUE-
ARE THE GOOD THINGS THAT YOU DO.

MY OBEDIENT HEART AND SOUL LEAP FOR JOY,
YOU SEE-
AS I BOW IN THE HOLY PRESENCE OF THE FOREVER-
LIVING GOD ALMIGHTY.

HOLY, HOLY, HOLY-
IS THE PRAISE WORTHY GOD ALMIGHTY!!!

LORD JESUS: IN THE MIDST OF YOUR DIVINITY-
MY BLESSED SOUL RECEIVES DIVINE PLEASURE
FROM GOD, THE FATHER, ALMIGHTY.

IT IS REAL! IT IS REAL! IT, GOD'S HOLY SPIRIT, IS
ETERNAL AND REAL!
IT IS A DIVINE LOVE THAT MY BLESSED SOUL CAN
TRULY SEE AND FEEL.

FOR, **HOLY AND TRUE**-
ARE THE HEAVEN SENT BLESSINGS THAT **COME FROM YOU.**

HOLY, HOLY, HOLY-
IS THE LIVING FIRST NOEL; GOD ALMIGHTY!!!

IN MY PEACEFUL ROOM OF DIVINE HEAVEN SENT HOPE

<u>**BARBARA SPEAKING**</u>

IN MY PEACEFUL ROOM OF **DIVINE HOPE**-
I WILL CLING TO THE GOD WHO **HELPS MY BLESSED SOUL COPE.**

IN MY ROOM OF DIVINE PEACEFUL **HOPE, YOU SEE**-
MY SOUL WILL UNITE WITH THE **FIRST NOEL; GOD ALMIGHTY.**

IN MY ROOM OF PEACEFUL HEAVEN **DESCENDED HOPE, YOU SEE**-
I WILL CLING TO THE TRUST AND LOVE THAT I HAVE FOR **CHRIST JESUS, THE ALMIGHTY.**

<u>**BARBARA SPEAKING TO CHRIST JESUS; THE FIRST HEAVEN SENT NOEL/CHRISTMAS**</u>

IN MY PEACEFUL ROOM OF HOPE, O BLESSED SAVIOR-
I WILL LOOK UP TO ALMIGHTY GOD, MY LIVING
REWARD AND ETERNAL FATHER.

IN MY ROOM OF DIVINE HOPE; IN MY ROOM OF DIVINE
HOPE: IN MY ROOM OF DIVINE LIVING HOPE, YOU SEE-
I WILL ALWAYS TRUST IN THE LOVE THAT DESCENDED
WITH THE FOREVER-LIVING CHRIST JESUS, THE
ALMIGHTY.

FOR, HOLY AND TRUE-
IS THE LOVE AND COMFORT THAT COME WITH
KNOWING WONDERFUL AND MAGNIFICENT YOU.

BARBARA SPEAKING

HOLY, HOLY, HOLY-
IS THE LIVING REALM CALLED CHRIST JESUS, THE
ALMIGHTY!!!

I WILL PLACE ALL OF MY SPIRITUAL AND PHYSICAL
TRUST IN CHRIST JESUS-
FOR, HE IS THE FOREVER-LIVING FIRST CHRISTMAS.

ALLELUIA! ALLELUIA! ALLELUIA-
TO THE ONLY BEGOTTEN SON OF ALMIGHTY GOD;
JEHOVAH!!!

PRAISE HIM! PRAISE HIM! **PRAISE, PRAISE, PRAISE!** PRAISE ALMIGHTY GOD, O BLESSED ONES, DURING THESE **PRAISEWORTHY DAYS!!!**

FOR, HE HAS DONE GREAT AND HOLY **WORKS IN OUR MIDST-**
AS HE REVEALS HIMSELF TO US, SO THAT THE BLESSED ONES **WILL KNOW THAT HE DOES EXIST.**

HOLY, HOLY, HOLY-
IS THE FIRST AND LAST LIVING NOEL ALMIGHTY!!!

HOLY, HOLY, HOLY-
IS THE FOREVER-LIVING CHRIST AND GOD ALMIGHTY!!!

I WILL ALWAYS TRUST AND FOLLOW CHRIST **JESUS, MY LIVING GOD AND SAVIOR-**
I WILL ALWAYS CLING TO THE LOVE AND GUIDANCE OF **ALMIGHTY GOD, MY ROYAL KING AND HEAVENLY FATHER.**

BARBARA SPEAKING TO THE LIVING GOD AND SAVIOR; CHRIST JESUS, THE ALMIGHTY

FOR, **HOLY AND TRUE-**
IS MY FAITH THAT **COMES FROM YOU.**

HOLY, HOLY, HOLY-
IS THE LOVE THAT COMES WITH KNOWING CHRIST
JESUS, THE ALMIGHTY!!!

IN YOUR ROOM OF HOPE

ALMIGHTY GOD SPEAKING TO EARTH'S INHABITANTS
TODAY

MY SWEET **LITTLE CHILDREN:**
YES! YOU FROM **EVERY BLESSED NATION.**

INTO YOUR WORLD OF HOPE **I WILL VISIT-**
AS I SHARE WITH YOU ALL, **MY HOLY DEVOTED
SPIRIT**

INTO YOUR WORLD OF **HOPE, YOU SEE-**
THE FIRST NOEL'S **DIVINE REALITY.**

FOR, **HOLY AND TRUE-**
IS THE FIRST CHRISTMAS (BABY JESUS) WHO TRULY
LOVES BLESSED YOU.

DEAR **CHILDREN-**
FROM EVERY **EARTHLY NATION.**

KEEP YOUR ROOM OF HOPE ALIVE, **DEAR SWEET
CHILDREN-**

Barbara Ann Mary Mack

SO THAT YOU MAY RECEIVE THE GIFT OF LIFE THAT
I GIVE TO **MY GREATEST CREATION.**

FOR, **HOLY AND TRUE-**
IS THE FIRST NOEL WHO **LOVES BLESSED YOU.**

HOLY, HOLY, HOLY-
IS THE FIRST EARTHLY CHRISTMAS CALLED CHRIST
JESUS, THE ALMIGHTY!!!

BARBARA SPEAKING

FOR, HE LOOKED UPON **HELPLESS NEEDY ME-**
A CHILD AND SERVANT OF **GOD, THE ALMIGHTY.**

HOLY AND TRUE-
IS THE GOD WHO LIVES WITH **BELOVED ME AND YOU.**

I WILL LOOK UPON **THE NEEDY CHILD-**
WHO REQUESTED MY ASSISTANCE **FOR A WHILE.**

I WILL LOOK UPON THE BEING OF CHRIST JESUS, OUR
NEW BORN KING OF KINGS-
WHO HAS COME TO EARTH AGAIN WITH **MANY
HEAVENLY GOOD THINGS.**

OH HOW **GRAND AND EXCITING-**

TO BE IN THE HOLY PRESENCE OF CHRIST **JESUS,**
OUR NEW BORN KING.

FOR, DURING **THIS HOLY NIGHT-**
CHRIST, THE NEW BORN KING, KEPT ME **WITHIN HIS**
HOLY SIGHT-

HOLY, HOLY, HOLY-
IS CHRIST JESUS; **HEAVEN AND EARTH'S NEW BORN**
BABY.

FOR, AT THE FATHER'S APPROVAL, **HE DID ENTER-**
THE OPEN GATES THAT LED TO EARTH'S **NEEDY SON**
AND DAUGHTER.

HOLY, HOLY, HOLY-
IS THE NEW BORN KING AND GOD ALMIGHTY!!!

<u>**CHRIST, THE NEW BORN KING, SPEAKING TO EARTH'S**</u>
<u>**INHABITANTS TODAY**</u>

DEAR **SWEET CHILDREN-**
ALL FROM EVERY **BLESSED NATION.**

I AM PRESENTLY **MOVING, YOU SEE-**
IN THE MIDST OF EARTH'S LOVED ONES WHO **BELONGS**
TO ROYAL ME.

Barbara Ann Mary Mack

FOR I, THE LORD JESUS-
MOVE IN THE MIDST OF THE SPIRITUALLY NEEDY
ONES AND THE RIGHTEOUS.

HOLY, HOLY, HOLY-
IS THE HEAVEN SENT NEW BORN BABE, CHRIST
JESUS, THE FOREVER-LIVING FIRST NOEL/
CHRISTMAS, ALMIGHTY!!!

BOOK # TWO

I NEED YOU, O LORD GOD

BY:

BARBARA ANN MARY MACK

I NEED YOU, O LORD GOD

BY:

BARBARA ANN MARY MACK

BEGAN: JULY 30, 2024

COMPLETED: JULY 31, 2024

I TRULY NEED YOU, O HOLY GOD AND FATHER

BARBARA SPEAKING TO ALMIGHTY GOD

I TRULY NEED YOU, O HOLY **GOD AND FATHER.**
HEAR THE HUMBLE PRAYERS OF YOUR OBEDIENT
MESSENGER AND DAUGHTER.

HEAR MY CRIES AND TEARS, FOR **THEY ARE MANY.**
HEAR MY HUMBLE CRIES AND PRAYERS, FOR THEY
ARE **OF THE NEEDY.**

HEAR ME-
HEAR THE CRIES OF THE WEEPING SERVANT OF **GOD
ALMIGHTY.**

FOR, MY WEEPING SOUL **IS IN NEED-**
OF THE HOLY GOD WHO **DOES FEED.**

FEED ME, **O HOLY GOD.**
FEED MY WEEPING SOUL FROM YOUR BASKET **OF
DIVINE LOVE.**

FOR, MY SOUL IS IN **DESPERATE NEED-**
OF THE GOD WHOSE HOLY **SPIRIT DOES FEED.**

COME. COME. COME TO ME **LORD JESUS.**

Barbara Ann Mary Mack

FILL MY WEEPING SOUL WITH THE FOOD THAT YOUR HOLY SPIRIT GIVES TO **THE FAITHFUL ONES AND THE RIGHTEOUS.**

COME, LORD JESUS, COME TO **YOUR NEEDY DAUGHTER-** COME TO ME WITH THE LOVE AND NOURISHMENT THAT ARE GIVEN TO YOUR **NEEDY FRIEND AND SENT MESSENGER.**

THE FAITHFUL ONES AND THE RIGHTEOUS

BARBARA SPEAKING TO THE LORD JESUS

COME, LORD JESUS. COME TO YOUR **NEEDY DAUGHTER.** COME WITH THE LOVE AND NOURISHMENT THAT ARE GIVEN TO **YOUR NEEDY FRIEND AND SENT MESSENGER.**

FOR MY CRIES **AT NIGHT-** HAVE REACHED YOUR **GLORIOUS SIGHT.**

COME, LORD GOD AND DIVINE **KING OF KINGS-** ENTER MY REALM OF NEED WITH YOUR **WONDERFUL HEAVENLY THINGS.**

COME, **O HOLY ONE.**

COME WITH THE GIFTS THAT FLOW FROM THE LIVING BEING AND ESSENCE OF GOD, THE **FATHER'S, ONLY BEGOTTEN SON.**

FOR, I AM IN NEED OF **YOUR DIVINE PRESENCE.** ENTER, LORD GOD. ENTER **MY EARTHLY RESIDENCE.**

SPEAK. SPEAK. SPEAK.
ENTER THE REALM OF NEED OF THE DAUGHTER WHOM **YOUR HOLY SPIRIT DOES SEEK.**

ENTER. ENTER. ENTER.
ENTER MY WEEPING SOUL, SO THAT YOUR HOLY PRESENCE MAY **COMFORT YOUR OBEDIENT DAUGHTER.**

ENTER MY **WEEPING SOUL TODAY.**
ENTER ME, LORD JESUS. JOIN MY WEEPING SPIRIT **AS I KNEEL AND PRAY.**

FOR, MY TROUBLED SPIRIT, SOUL, **AND WEAK BODY-** NEED THE DIVINE ASSISTANCE OF **GOD ALMIGHTY.**

COME, LORD JESUS. COME TO YOUR OBEDIENT **MESSENGER TODAY.**
COME, O HOLY GOD, AND ENTER MY BLESSED SOUL AS MY VALUABLE **SPIRIT AND BODY PRAY.**

Barbara Ann Mary Mack

COME TO ME IN THE **MIDDLE OF THE NIGHT-**
AS YOU KEEP YOUR WOUNDED DAUGHTER WITHIN
YOUR GLORIOUS SIGHT.

FOR, MY BLESSED **SOUL DOES NEED-**
THE HOLY GOD AND SAVIOR **WHO DOES FEED.**

LOOK UPON YOUR **TRUSTING DAUGHTER.**
LOOK UPON THE NEEDY SOUL THAT BELONGS TO
ALMIGHTY GOD, OUR HEAVENLY FATHER.

FOR, HE **DOES CARE-**
ABOUT THE WEEPING SOUL WHOSE **HEART IS VERY
NEAR.**

WEEP WITH ME, **KING JESUS.**
WEEP WITH THE VULNERABLE DAUGHTER OF
ALMIGHTY GOD, **THE HEAVEN SENT RIGHTEOUS.**

FOR, **HOLY AND TRUE-**
IS THE LORD AND GOD WHO SEES MY **WEEPING SOUL
THROUGH.**

**MAKE WAY! MAKE WAY! MAKE WAY FOR ALMIGHTY
GOD'S WEEPING DAUGHTER!**

BARBARA SPEAKING

MAKE WAY FOR ALMIGHTY GOD'S WEEPING DAUGHTER.
MAKE WAY FOR THE FAITHFUL AND OBEDIENT HEAVEN SENT MESSENGER!

FOR, MY FAITHFULNESS-
GIVES ALLEGIANCE TO GOD, THE FATHER'S, REALM OF HOLINESS.

HOLY, HOLY, HOLY-
IS ALMIGHTY GOD'S REALM OF INFINITY.

BARBARA SPEAKING TO ALMIGHTY GOD, THE FATHER

HOLY IS YOUR ETERNAL NAME, DEAR FATHER GOD.
EVERLASTING IS YOUR CONTINUOUS DEVOTION AND LOVE.

DEAR FATHER-
HELP BARBARA, YOUR WEEPING FRIEND AND DEVOTED DAUGHTER.

FOR, MY REALM OF NEED HAS REACHED YOUR HOLY EARS-
AND NOW, YOUR HOLY SPIRIT AND PRESENCE WILL SHARE MY MANY FALLING PROTECTED TEARS.

FOR, **HOLY AND TRUE-**
ARE THE FALLING TEARS THAT I **HAVE SHARED**
WITH YOU.

HOLY, HOLY, HOLY-
ARE THE FALLING TEARS OF BARBARA AND GOD
ALMIGHTY!!!

FOR, THROUGH **THE MANY YEARS-**
ALMIGHTY GOD'S HOLY HANDS HAVE **CAUGHT MY**
FALLEN TEARS.

IN MY REALM OF NEED, MY WEEPING SOUL WAITS
FOR THE HEAVENLY HOLY ONE

<u>BARBARA SPEAKING</u>

WITHIN MY REALM OF SPIRITUAL **NEED, YOU SEE-**
MY IGNITED SOUL WAITS FOR THE DIVINE PRESENCE
OF **GOD, THE ALMIGHTY.**

FOR, HIS HOLY SPIRIT AND **PRESENCE, YOU SEE-**
DO COMFORT **WEEPING ME.**

FOR, HIS **HOLY PRESENCE-**
SURROUNDS MY **WELCOMING RESIDENCE.**

HOLY, HOLY, HOLY-

IS THE WELCOMED PRESENCE OF GOD ALMIGHTY!!!

WITH MY SPIRITUAL ARMS OPEN WIDE-
I WILL RELEASE A LOVE THAT MY OBEDIENT BEING
CANNOT HIDE.

FOR, ALMIGHTY GOD'S PRESENCE AND HOLINESS-
OPEN THE GATES TO HIS REALM OF HEAVEN SENT
GOODNESS.

FOR, HOLY, YOU SEE-
IS THE GOODNESS OF GOD, THE FATHER, ALMIGHTY.

BARBARA SPEAKING TO ALMIGHTY GOD, THE
FATHER

YOU ARE GOOD TO ME, DEAR HEAVENLY GOD OF
ALL TIME.
EVERYTHING THAT IS HOLY, IS YOURS AND MINE.

HOLY, HOLY, HOLY-
IS THE GOODNESS OF GOD ALMIGHTY!!!

FOR, YOU, O HOLY GOD-
REIGN IN THE MIDST OF MY DEVOTION AND LOVE.
AS YOU SEND DOWN YOUR MANY BLESSINGS FROM
SWEET HEAVEN ABOVE.

Barbara Ann Mary Mack

HOLY, HOLY, HOLY-
IS MY HEAVEN SENT HELPER; GOD, THE ALMIGHTY!!!

I WILL **REACH, YOU SEE**-
FOR THE HOLY GOD WHO BRINGS COMFORT, DIVINE
PEACE, AND **JOY TO BLESSED ME.**

HELP ME, DEAR LORD JESUS

BARBARA SPEAKING TO THE HEAVEN SENT LORD JESUS; OUR SAVING GOD AND FRIEND

HELP ME, LORD JESUS. HELP YOUR **OBEDIENT
SERVANT TODAY.**
HELP ME, O LORD GOD, AS I LEAD YOUR EARTHLY
LOVED ONES TO YOUR LIFE SAVING **AND REWARDING
HOLY WAY.**

FOR, **HOLY AND TRUE**-
IS MY UNENDING **LOVE FOR YOU.**

MY **DEVOTION**-
IS FOR THE GOD AND CREATOR OF HIS **OBEDIENT
EARTHLY CHILDREN.**

I ADORE **YOUR HOLINESS**-
I BOW IN THE PRESENCE OF **YOUR GREATNESS.**

HOLY, HOLY, HOLY-
IS MY LOVE FOR GOD ALMIGHTY!!!

LET THE HEAVENLY BELLS RING!!!

BARBARA SPEAKING

THE HEAVENLY **BELLS RING-**
AS MY BODY AND SOUL BOW IN THE MIDST OF
ALMIGHTY GOD, MY GREAT AND **WORTHY HEAVEN
SENT KING.**

FOR, **HOLY, YOU SEE-**
IS THE GREAT GOD WHO CALLED INTO EXISTENCE
BLESSED ME.

HOLY, HOLY, HOLY-
IS THE LIVING SPIRIT OF CHRIST ALMIGHTY!!!

FOR, HE MOVES AND **REIGNS IN MY MIDST-**
AS I REVEAL THE TRUST THAT **HE DOES EXIST.**

FOR, **HOLY, YOU SEE-**
IS THE EXISTING GOD WHO **NEEDS BLESSED ME.**

FOR, HE SENDS TO HIS EARTHLY LOVED **ONES,
YOU SEE-**

THE FAITHFUL MESSENGER AND DAUGHTER OF THE FOREVER-LIVING GOD ALMIGHTY.

BARBARA SPEAKING TO CHRIST JESUS, OUR LIFE SAVING GOD AND KING

COME, O **BLESSED SAVIOR**-
DINE WITH ME TODAY, FOR I AM YOUR FAITHFUL AND **OBEDIENT DAUGHTER.**

DINE WITH ME IN THE MIDST OF **YOUR HEAVENLY JOY**-
AS I REVEAL YOUR DIVINE TRUTH TO **EVERY WEEPING GIRL AND BOY.**

HOLY, HOLY, HOLY-
IS THE WELCOMED PRESENCE OF CHRIST JESUS, THE ALMIGHTY!!!

AND HE, CHRIST JESUS; ALMIGHTY GOD, CAUGHT MY FALLEN TEARS TODAY

ALMIGHTY GOD SPEAKING TO BARBARA TODAY

I HAVE CAUGHT THEM TODAY, **DEAR BARBARA.**
I HAVE CAUGHT THE FALLEN TEARS OF MY FAITHFUL **MESSENGER AND DAUGHTER.**

ALTHOUGH THEY **WERE MANY**-

YOUR FALLEN TEARS HAVE BEEN STORED WITHIN THE **DEVOTED HEART OF GOD ALMIGHTY.**

FOR, **HOLY AND TRUE-**
IS THE GOD WHO SITS NEXT TO BELOVED **AND BLESSED YOU.**

HOLY, HOLY, HOLY-
ARE THE FALLEN TEARS THAT BELONG TO THE FAITHFUL DAUGHTER AND MESSENGER OF CHRIST JESUS, THE ALMIGHTY!!!

MY FALLEN TEARS HAVE JOINED ALMIGHTY GOD ON HIS HEAVENLY THRONE ON HIGH

BARBARA SPEAKING

THEY, MY FALLEN TEARS, HAVE **GATHERED, YOU SEE-**
AROUND THE LIVING THRONE OF **GOD ALMIGHTY.**

THEY HAVE **JOINED, YOU SEE-**
THE HEAVENLY RESIDENTS THAT BELONG TO **THE ETERNAL GOD ALMIGHTY.**

MY TEARS, MY TEARS; MY **MANY FALLEN TEARS-**

WILL DANCE IN THE HOLY PRESENCE OF ALMIGHTY
GOD **THROUGHOUT THE HEAVENLY UNENDING
YEARS.**

FOR, **HOLY, YOU SEE-**
ARE THE MANY TEARS THAT FELL FROM THE
WEEPING EYES OF **THE MESSENGER OF GOD
ALMIGHTY.**

HOLY, HOLY, HOLY-
ARE THE TEARS THAT BELONG TO THE DAUGHTER
OF GOD ALMIGHTY!!!

FALL! FALL! FALL, O BLESSED TEARS OF MINE!

BARBARA SPEAKING

FALL. FALL. FALL, O BLESSED **TEARS OF MINE.**
FOR, YOU WILL TRAVEL WITH ALMIGHTY GOD
THROUGHOUT **THE REALM OF UNENDING TIME.**

TRAVEL WITH **THE HOLY SPIRIT-**
MAKE A JOYOUS SOUND, SO THAT THE RESIDENTS
OF HEAVEN AND EARTH **WILL HEAR IT.**

MAKE A JOYOUS AND **MELODIOUS SOUND-**
SO THAT HEAVEN'S BLESSED RESIDENTS WILL
KNOW THAT **YOU ARE AROUND.**

SING, O BLESSED TEARS OF **MINE, SING!**
REJOICE TODAY, FOR YOU ARE IN THE HOLY PRESENCE
OF **CHRIST JESUS, OUR MIGHTY VICTORIOUS GOD
AND KING.**

RING! RING! RING, O BLESSED BELLS OF **HEAVENLY
DIVINE LOVE!**
JOIN MY REJOICING TEARS, IN THE PRESENCE OF
OUR HOLY GOD ABOVE.

FOR, HE BRINGS **THE KIND OF JOY-**
THAT THE GATES OF HELL **CAN NEVER DESTROY.**

RING, O BLESSED BELLS! **RING LOUD AND CLEAR-**
RING, O BLESSED HEAVENLY BELLS, FOR YOU ARE
IN THE PRESENCE OF THE MIGHTY SAVING **GOD WHO
IS VERY NEAR.**

FOR, **HOLY AND TRUE-**
IS THE GOD WHO **FORMED YOU.**

**AND MY FALLEN TEARS DID ENTER GOD'S HEAVENLY
RESIDENCE ABOVE**

BARBARA SPEAKING TO HER FALLEN TEARS

REJOICE, O BLESSED FALLEN **TEARS OF MINE!**

Barbara Ann Mary Mack

FOR, YOU WILL SHARE GOD'S THRONE OF MERCY DURING THIS **MERCY SEEKING PERIOD OF TIME.**

YOU WILL JOIN CHRIST JESUS, THE MIGHTY **LIVING KING OF KINGS-**
AS HE PROCLAIMS HIS GREATNESS, AS HE SHARES WITH US, **HIS HEAVEN SENT GOOD TIDINGS.**

REJOICE! REJOICE! REJOICE! REJOICE IN THE MIDST **OF DIVINE GLORY!**
REJOICE, O BLESSED TEARS OF MINE! FOR, YOU ARE A VERY VALUABLE PART OF **HIS HOLY UNENDING LOVE STORY.**

REJOICE IN THE PRESENCE OF **DIVINE GLADNESS-**
AS YOU BECOME ENVELOPED IN **HIS HOLY LOVE STORY.**

FOR, **HOLY, YOU SEE-**
IS GOD'S **UNENDING LOVE STORY.**

HOLY, HOLY, HOLY-
IS ALMIGHTY GOD, THE KING OF UNENDING GLORY!!!

THE HEAVENLY GATES HAVE OPENED WIDE

BARBARA SPEAKING

THE HEAVENLY GATES HAVE **OPENED WIDE-**
FOR, THEY WELCOME MY MANY FALLEN TEARS
THAT I **COULD NOT HIDE.**

YOU, O BLESSED FALLEN TEARS OF MINE, HAVE
BEEN WELCOMED INTO GOD'S **ETERNAL HOME OF
DIVINE LOVE.**
YES, SWEET **HEAVEN ABOVE!**

ENTER THROUGH HEAVEN'S OPEN GATES, **O
BLESSED TEARS!**
FOR YOU WILL DWELL IN SWEET PARADISE THROUGH
GOD'S BLESSED **UNENDING YEARS.**

AND NOW, O BLESSED **FALLEN TEARS OF MINE-**
YOU WILL RESIDE WITH GOD, THE FATHER,
THROUGHOUT THE REALM OF **UNENDING PRICELESS
TIME.**

HOLY, HOLY, HOLY-
IS THE HEAVENLY RESIDENCE THAT HOUSES GOD
ALMIGHTY!!!

HOLY, HOLY, HOLY, **IS THE RESIDENCE-**
THAT HOUSES ALMIGHTY **GOD'S INFINITE
PRESENCE!!!**

DIVINE LOVE-

Barbara Ann Mary Mack

DESCENDS FROM **SWEET HEAVEN ABOVE.**

FOR, HIS **DIVINE GLORY-**
REVEALS HIS **UNENDING LOVE STORY.**

MOVE IN THE DIRECTION OF DIVINE LOVE, **O SWEET FLOWING TEARS.**
FOR, YOU WILL NOW RESIDE WITH YOUR SAVIOR AND GOD THROUGHOUT SWEET **ETERNITY'S UNENDING REJOICING YEARS.**

HOLY, HOLY, HOLY-
ARE THE FALLEN TEARS THAT DWELL WITH GOD ALMIGHTY!!!

MY REALM OF NEED HAS **RELEASED THE TEARS-**
THAT WILL ACCOMPANY OUR SAVING GOD DURING **THESE PRAISE WORTHY YEARS.**

HOLY, HOLY, HOLY-
ARE THE PRAISE WORTHY TEARS THAT ACCOMPANY THE **FOREVER REIGNING GOD ALMIGHTY!!!**

HOLY, HOLY, HOLY-
IS THE PRAISE WORTHY GOD ALMIGHTY!!!

FOR, THE REALM OF SPIRITUAL **NEED, YOU SEE-**

HAS BEEN SATISFIED BY THE HOLY PRESENCE OF THE FOREVER-LIVING GOD ALMIGHTY.

FOR, DIVINE SATISFACTION-
HAS SURROUNDED THE FALLEN TEARS OF BARBARA, GOD'S GREAT CREATION.

HOLY, HOLY, HOLY-
IS THE SATISFIED DAUGHTER OF GOD ALMIGHTY!!!

AND THEN, MY FALLEN TEARS, BOWED IN ALMIGHTY GOD'S HOLY PRESENCE

BARBARA SPEAKING

I OBSERVE, YOU SEE-
THE MANY TEARS THAT FELL FROM THE OBEDIENT EYES OF THE MESSENGER OF GOD ALMIGHTY.

FOR, IN HIS HOLY PRESENCE-
MY WELCOMED FALLEN TEARS ENTERED HIS HEAVENLY RESIDENCE.

HOLY, HOLY, HOLY-
IS THE HEAVENLY RESIDENCE OF GOD ALMIGHTY!!!

BOW! BOW! BOW, O BLESSED TEARS OF MINE!

Barbara Ann Mary Mack

BOW IN THE HOLY PRESENCE OF GOD ALMIGHTY, DURING **THIS PRECIOUS PERIOD OF TIME.**

FOR, YOU HAVE BEEN BLESSED, **O PRECIOUS TEARS.** ENJOY! ENJOY! ENJOY OUR SAVING GOD THROUGHOUT **THESE UNENDING YEARS!**

FOR, **HOLY, YOU SEE-** IS THE GOD WHO **DWELLS WITHIN ME.**

HE MOVES, **YOU SEE-** WITHIN MY PURIFIED AND **SANCTIFIED BODY.**

HOLY, YOU SEE- IS THE HEAVEN SENT KING WHO GOVERNS OVER HIS EARTHLY **LOVED ONES AND ME.**

BARBARA SPEAKING TO CHRIST JESUS, OUR LIFE SAVING GOD AND ROYAL KING

REJOICE, O GREAT RESCUING **LIFE-SAVING GOD!** EXHIBIT YOUR REALM OF SATISFACTION **AND DIVINE LOVE.**

FOR, YOU HAVE BROUGHT **SATISFACTION, YOU SEE-** TO THE NEEDY DAUGHTER OF **GOD ALMIGHTY.**

OH HOLY TEARS

BARBARA SPEAKING TO GOD'S FALLEN TEARS

OH HOLY TEARS-

THAT HAVE FALLEN FROM GOD'S BLESSED EYES
THROUGH THE YEARS.

FOR, ALMIGHTY GOD, YOU SEE-
HAS RELEASED MANY TEARS OVER THE HARDSHIP
OF HIS EARTHLY LOVED ONES AND ME.

FOR, THROUGH THE MANY YEARS, YOU SEE-
OUR GOD HAS WITNESSED OUR MANY SINS, WHICH
IS A TRAGEDY.

FOR, HOLY, YOU SEE-
IS THE GOD AND DIVINE SAVIOR WHO HAS WEPT FOR
YOU AND ME.

HOLY, HOLY, HOLY-
IS THE WEEPING GOD ALMIGHTY!!!

FOR, THE MANY TEARS THAT HE DID SHED, YOU SEE-
BROUGHT ABOUT SALVATION AND REPENTANCE
FOR HIS SINFUL CHILDREN AND ME.

HOLY, HOLY, HOLY-
ARE THE TEARS THAT FELL FROM THE ESSENCE
AND BEING OF GOD ALMIGHTY!!!

FOR, OUR MANY **SINS, YOU SEE-**
BROKE THE SPIRITUAL HEART OF GOD, OUR
HEAVENLY FATHER ALMIGHTY.

HOLY, HOLY, HOLY-
IS THE COMPASSIONATE AND **MERCIFUL GOD**
ALMIGHTY!!!

FOR, HIS FALLEN **TEARS, YOU SEE-**
REVEALED HIS DIVINE **COMPASSION AND MERCY.**

FOR, ALMIGHTY GOD, **THE MERCIFUL ONE-**
DID SHED MANY TEARS OVER THE SINFUL ACTS OF
HIS **EARTHLY DAUGHTER AND SON.**

HOLY, HOLY, HOLY-
ARE THE MANY TEARS THAT FELL FROM THE
SPIRITUAL EYES OF OUR WEEPING GOD ALMIGHTY!!!

MY HOLY TEARS **HAVE AWAKEN-**
IN THE HOLY PRESENCE OF ALMIGHTY GOD AND **HIS**
HEAVENLY CREATION.

THEY NOW, MOVE AROUND **HIS MIGHTY THRONE-**
IN THE PRESENCE OF THE HOLY ONE WHO IS **NEVER**
ALONE.

MOVE, O BLESSED TEARS OF MINE, FOR, YOU ARE
NEVER ALONE.
MOVE, O BLESSED TEARS OF MINE. MOVE AROUND
GOD'S MIGHTY THRONE.

FOR, ALMIGHTY GOD, YOU SEE-
HAS PROMISED THAT HE WOULD ALWAYS DWELL
WITHIN BLESSED ME.

FOR, HOLY AND TRUE-
IS THE GOD WHO SURROUNDS ME AND YOU.

HOLY, HOLY, HOLY-
IS THE VISIBLE PRESENCE OF CHRIST ALMIGHTY!!!

FOR, HE DOES EXIST-
IN MY FALLEN TEARS MIDST.

HOLY, HOLY, HOLY-
IS THE VISIBLE PRESENCE OF CHRIST JESUS, THE
ALMIGHTY!!!

FOR, HE HAS BLESSED AND RECEIVED, YOU SEE-
THE MANY FALLEN TEARS THAT BELONG TO ME.

HOLY, HOLY, HOLY-
ARE THE MANY FALLEN TEARS OF GOD ALMIGHTY!!!

Barbara Ann Mary Mack

FOR, IN HIS HOLY MIDST-
HIS ESSENCE AND BEING DO EXIST.

HOLY, HOLY, HOLY-
IS THE VISIBLE PRESENCE OF GOD, THE ALMIGHTY!!!

HOME. HOME. HOME AT LAST

BARBARA SPEAKING

HOME. HOME. HOME AT LAST!
I WILL SHOUT HALLELUJAH, BECAUSE MY MANY
FALLEN TEARS ARE OF THE PAST.

FOR, ALMIGHTY GOD, YOU SEE-
HAS CAPTURED THE PROBLEMS THAT ONCE
WORRIED ME.

HOLY, HOLY, HOLY-
IS THE SALVATION OF CHRIST ALMIGHTY!!!

FOR, MY FALLEN TEARS, YOU SEE-
NOW DWELL IN THE SACRED HOME OF CHRIST JESUS,
THE ALMIGHTY.

HOLY, HOLY, HOLY, AND REAL-
IS THE COMFORTING PRESENCE OF ALMIGHTY GOD
THAT MY BLESSED SOUL CAN TRULY FEEL!!!

THE DOOR TO MY REALM OF NEED HAS BEEN OFFICIALLY CLOSED

BARBARA SPEAKING

THE DOOR TO MY REALM OF NEED HAS BEEN OFFICIALLY CLOSED, YOU SEE-
BY THE DIVINE POWER OF OUR MERCIFUL GOD ALMIGHTY.

FOR, HE HAS SATISFIED AND FULFILLED ALL OF MY WORLDLY AND SPIRITUAL NEEDS, YOU SEE-
AND NOW, MY BLESSED SPIRIT RESIDES COMFORTABLY IN THE CARE OF THE BLESSED HOLY TRINITY.

FOR, GOD, THE FATHER-
TAKES VERY GOOD CARE OF HIS FAITHFUL DAUGHTER; OBEDIENT BARBARA.

HOLY, HOLY, HOLY-
IS THE REALM THAT HOUSES GOD ALMIGHTY.

FOR, HE HAS SATISFIED ALL OF MY EARTHLY NEEDS, YOU SEE-
WITH THE LOVE THAT COMES FROM HIS REALM OF INFINITY.

Barbara Ann Mary Mack

BARBARA SPEAKING TO ALMIGHTY GOD, THE FATHER

DEAR HOLY **FATHER ABOVE-**
YOU HAVE GRACED YOUR DAUGHTER, BARBARA,
WITH THE GIFTS THAT CAME FROM YOUR **MIGHTY THRONE OF UNENDING LOVE.**

YOUR **DEVOTION-**
SURROUNDS YOUR BLESSED **EARTHLY CREATION.**

FOR, I TRULY **ADORE, YOU SEE-**
THE HOLY ONE WHO COMFORTS YOUR BLESSED
EARTHLY **LOVED ONES AND ME.**

YOUR **REALM OF LOVE-**
SURROUNDS ME, AS I LOOK UP TOWARDS **SWEET HEAVEN ABOVE.**

OH WHAT A **BLESSED DELIGHT-**
TO BEHOLD YOUR DIVINE **STRENGTH AND MIGHT.**

HOLY IS THE REALM THAT **YOU RELEASE-**
AS YOUR CHILDREN AND I CLING TO YOUR **HEAVEN DESCENDED PEACE.**

YOUR HOLY PRESENCE **DOES EXIST-**

FOR, YOU WALK WITH ME, AS I WALK IN YOUR
EARTHLY LOVED ONES BLESSED MIDST.

HOLY, HOLY, HOLY-
IS THE VISIBLE PRESENCE OF THE HEAVEN
DESCENDED GOD ALMIGHTY!!!

AS OUR WOUNDED SOULS CRY OUT TO GOD ALMIGHTY
THROUGHOUT THE NIGHT

BARBARA SPEAKING

MY WOUNDED SOUL CRIES OUT TO MY SAVING GOD
THROUGHOUT THE NIGHT.
FOR, WE LONG TO BEHOLD HIS GLORIOUS SHINING
LIGHT.

FOR, ONLY HE-
CAN BRING COMFORT TO HIS LOVED ONES AND ME.

HOLY, HOLY, HOLY, YOU SEE-
IS THE LIGHT THAT EMITS FROM THE HOLY SPIRIT
OF GOD ALMIGHTY!!!

BARBARA SPEAKING TO ALMIGHTY GOD, THE
FATHER

YOU, O LOVING GOD-

TRANSCENDS ALL FORMS OF **MANMADE LOVE.**

OH HOW **GRAND–**
TO WITNESS THE PHYSICAL TOUCH OF GOD
ALMIGHTY'S **HOLY ETERNAL HAND.**

HOLY IS YOUR ETERNAL **NAME, DEAR ONE.**
UNENDING PRAISE ARE ON THE LIPS OF YOUR
GRATEFUL DAUGHTER AND SON.

FOR, HOLY AND **ETERNAL, YOU SEE–**
ARE THE UNENDING PRAISE THAT FLOWS FROM THE
CHILDREN OF CHRIST ALMIGHTY.

PRAISE! PRAISE! **CONTINUOUS GLORIOUS PRAISE–**
ACCOMPANIES THESE **WORSHIPPING DAYS!**

FOR, ALMIGHTY **GOD, YOU SEE–**
IS WORTHY OF THE UNENDING PRAISE THAT COMES
FROM **HIS GRATEFUL CHILDREN AND ME.**

AND WHEN WE CALL OUT TO THE LORD JESUS IN OUR
TIMES OF SPIRITUAL AND PHYSICAL NEED

BARBARA SPEAKING TO THE LORD JESUS

HELP US. HELP US–

HELP US, O GRACIOUS AND **COMPASSIONATE LORD JESUS.**

HELP YOUR **NEEDY CHILDREN.**
GIVE PEACE AND JOY TO YOUR **GREATEST CREATION.**

FOR, WE ARE IN **NEED, YOU SEE-**
OF THE LOVE AND MERCY THAT COME WITH KNOWING **THE FOREVER-LIVING CHRIST JESUS; THE ALMIGHTY.**

ALL OF OUR SPIRITUAL AND PHYSICAL NEEDS ARE **MET, YOU SEE-**
BY THE REALM OF LOVE CALLED **GOD ALMIGHTY.**

FOR, **HE KNOWS-**
WHERE ALL OF **HIS CHILDREN GOES.**

HE **SEEKS, YOU SEE-**
THE NEEDS OF THOSE WHO **BELONG TO GOD ALMIGHTY.**

HIS HOLY SPIRIT IS **EVERYWHERE-**
HE SHOWS ALL OF US THAT THE LORD **JESUS REALLY DOES CARE.**

FOR, **HOLY AND TRUE-**
IS THE GOD WHO SHOWS MERCY TOWARD **ME AND YOU.**

Barbara Ann Mary Mack

FOR, OUR SPIRITUAL AND PHYSICAL **NEEDS, YOU SEE-**
ARE SATISFIED BY THE DIVINE POWER OF THE
OMNIPOTENT ONE; **GOD, THE ALMIGHTY.**

HOLY, HOLY, HOLY, AND REAL-
IS THE HEAVENLY POWER THAT **THE BELIEVING
ONES WILL FEEL!!!**

DIVINE HELP IS ON THE WAY, SAYS THE LORD JESUS

**THE LORD JESUS SPEAKING TO EARTH'S RESIDENTS
TODAY**

DEAR **LITTLE CHILDREN-**
I AM ON MY WAY TO HELP **MY GREATEST CREATION.**

FOR, I HAVE HEARD THE SOUNDS OF **YOUR CRIES,
YOU SEE-**
FOR, THEY HAVE REACHED THE THRONE OF THE
FOREVER-**LIVING KING ALMIGHTY.**

HELP IS **ON THE WAY-**
FOR, I HAVE HEARD YOUR MANY TEARS AS YOUR
HURTING SPIRITS DID PRAY.

FOR, **HOLY AND TRUE-**
IS THE GOD WHO HAS **COME BACK TO SAVE
BLESSED YOU.**

I CAN HEAR THE HOLY VOICE AND SPIRIT OF MY
HEAVEN SENT GOD AND HELPER

BARBARA SPEAKING TO ALMIGHTY GOD, EARTH'S
RESIDENTS DIVINE HELPER TODAY

I CAN HEAR YOU, O DIVINE HELPER.
I CAN REALLY HEAR THE HOLY VOICE AND SPIRIT
OF CHRIST JESUS, MY HEAVEN SENT HELPER AND
SAVIOR.

I CAN HEAR YOU-
I CAN HEAR THE VOICE OF HE WHO IS HOLY, ETERNAL
AND TRUE.

I CAN REALLY HEAR YOU, O DIVINE ONE.
I CAN HEAR THE MAGNIFICENT VOICE OF GOD, THE
FATHER'S, ONLY BEGOTTEN SON.

FOR, YOU, O HOLY ONE, HAVE A VOICE THAT TRAVELS
AND TRANSCENDS IN THE MIDST OF US.
YES, INDEED! I DO HEAR THE VOICE OF THE LIVING
CHRIST JESUS.

FOR, YOUR HOLY SPIRIT AND PRESENCE MOVE ME-
YES, DEAR GOD! YOUR HOLY ESSENCE MOVES THE
DAUGHTER AND MESSENGER (BARBARA) OF GOD
ALMIGHTY.

HOLY IS YOUR VISIBLE PRESENCE, LORD JESUS

BARBARA SPEAKING TO THE LORD JESUS

HOLY IS YOUR VISIBLE **PRESENCE, LORD JESUS-**
ETERNAL IS THE GOD AND DIVINE KING WHO HAS
COME TO BACK TO SAVE **THE FAITHFUL ONES AND
THE RIGHTEOUS.**

HOLY IS YOUR **PRESENCE, MY SAVIOR.**
GREAT AND MERCIFUL IS OUR HEAVENLY **GOD AND
FATHER.**

FOR, HE SENT YOU AGAIN **TO HELP US.**
YES! JEHOVAH GOD SENT THE FOREVER-**LIVING
CHRIST JESUS.**

HELP **US-**
LORD **JESUS.**

HELP YOUR SPIRITUALLY BLIND CHILDREN: **HELP US-
LORD JESUS.**

FOR, WE **ARE SINKING-**
IN THE VISIBLE PRESENCE OF OUR HOLY SAVIOR,
GOD, **AND DIVINE KING.**

HELP YOUR SINKING **LOVED ONES.**

LORD JESUS: HELP YOUR VULNERABLE DAUGHTERS
AND SONS.

FOR, OUR SOULS DO NEED–
THE HEAVENLY FOOD THAT ONLY YOU CAN PROVIDE
AND FEED.

WE ARE IN NEED, DEAR GOD AND FATHER.
YOUR CHILDREN NEED THE CONSTANT CARE OF A
HOLY GOD AND FATHER WHO IS ALWAYS THERE FOR
HIS WOUNDED SON AND DAUGHTER.

YOUR CHILDREN NEED THE CONSTANT CARE–
OF A HOLY GOD WHO IS ALWAYS NEAR.

FEED US. FEED US.
FEED US, O BLESSED LORD JESUS.

YOUR DESCENDED HOLY WORDS ARE THE
NOURISHMENT THAT YOUR CHILDREN NEED,
LORD GOD.
FEED US, LORD JESUS, WITH YOUR BASKET OF
DIVINE LOVE.

FOR, HOLY AND TRUE–
ARE THE WORDS OF LOVE THAT COME FROM
BLESSED YOU.

Barbara Ann Mary Mack

THE FOOD OF EVERLASTING LIFE HAS CAPTURED ME

BARBARA SPEAKING

THE HEAVEN SENT FOOD OF EVERLASTING LIFE
HAS CAPTURED ME.
I HAVE BEEN CAPTURED BY THE HOLY PRESENCE
OF CHRIST JESUS, THE ALMIGHTY.

BEHOLD, DEAR BROTHERS AND SISTERS

BARBARA SPEAKING TO EARTH'S NEEDY RESIDENTS

BEHOLD, DEAR BROTHERS AND BLESSED SISTERS,
FOR THE LORD JESUS HAS RISEN.
IN THE MIDST OF HIS NEEDY CHILDREN.

HE HAS COME BACK TO HELP US-
AND NOW, WE MAY BEHOLD THE HOLY PRESENCE OF
THE LIVING CHRIST JESUS.

HOLY, HOLY, HOLY-
IS HIS ETERNAL NAME; CHRIST JESUS, THE
ALMIGHTY!!!

HIS ETERNAL NAME-

REVEALS HIS WORLD OF DIVINE ROYALTY AND FAME.

HOLY AND ETERNAL ARE MY GOD'S REALM OF DIVINE LOVE.
MERCIFUL AND COMPASSIONATE IS THE SAVIOR WHO DESCENDED TO EARTH'S NEEDY ONES IN THE MIDST OF THE HEAVENLY CLOUDS ABOVE.

HOLY, HOLY, HOLY-
IS THE HEAVEN SENT CHRIST ALMIGHTY!!!

FOR, HE DESCENDED, YOU SEE-
IN THE HOLY PRESENCE OF GOD, THE FATHER, ALMIGHTY.

DESCEND TO ME, LORD JESUS

BARBARA SPEAKING TO THE RISEN CHRIST JESUS

DESCEND TO ME-
LET ME BEHOLD THE BEAUTY OF THE DESCENDED CHRIST ALMIGHTY.

DESCEND TO YOUR NEEDY ONES, O GREAT AND HOLY GOD-
GUIDE ME TO MY NEEDY BROTHERS AND SISTERS, LORD JESUS; GOD OF CONTINUOUS DIVINE LOVE.

GUIDE ME TO MY NEEDY BROTHERS AND SISTERS,
LORD JESUS.
GUIDE TO THE REALM THAT HOUSES YOUR TRUSTING
ONES AND THE RIGHTEOUS.

FOR, HOLY AND TRUE-
IS THE DESCENDED HELP THAT COMES WITH YOU.

DIVINE LOVE HAS ENTERED EARTH'S NEEDY REALM
AGAIN.
HE HAS RETURNED, SO THAT HE MAY REMOVE
EARTH'S RESIDENTS CONTINUOUS SUFFERING AND
PAIN.

DIVINITY HAS ENTERED MY
EARTHLY HOME AGAIN

BARBARA SPEAKING

ALMIGHTY GOD, SWEET DIVINITY-
HAS ENTERED THE EARTHLY HOME OF BARBARA,
THE SENT MESSENGER OF CHRIST ALMIGHTY.

SWEET DIVINITY-
HAS ENTERED THE GREAT CREATION CALLED
HUMANITY.

HE ENTERED WITHOUT WARNING-

HE ENTERED EARTH'S REALM WITH THE BLESSINGS OF THE LIVING CHRIST **JESUS, THE HEAVENLY LOVING KING.**

HOLY IS **HIS NAME**- SWEET ETERNITY IS HIS **REALM OF SPIRITUAL FAME.**

HOLY, HOLY, HOLY- IS THE FOREVER-LIVING CHRIST ALMIGHTY!!!

WHEN MY BLESSED SOUL NEEDS YOU, O LORD GOD

BARBARA SPEAKING TO ALMIGHTY GOD

O LORD GOD: WHEN MY NEEDY SOUL **CRIES OUT TO YOU**- I LOOK FOR A LOVE THAT IS **HOLY, ETERNAL AND TRUE.**

WHEN I LOOK UP TOWARD **SWEET HEAVEN**- I LOOK FOR THE HOLY ONE WHO CALLED INTO EXISTENCE, **HIS GREATEST CREATION.**

WHEN I NEED DIVINE HELP FROM **BLESSED ETERNAL YOU**- I LOOK BEYOND THE MANY STARS FOR THE SPIRIT OF HE WHO **SEES HIS EARTHLY LOVED ONES THROUGH.**

Barbara Ann Mary Mack

OH, HOW HOLY YOU ARE, **O GREAT ONE**-
FOR, YOU TRULY ARE THE DIVINE ORIGIN OF YOUR
NEEDY AND **GRATEFUL DAUGHTER AND SON.**

O HELPFUL **GREAT ONE**-
O FAITHFUL **ONLY BEGOTTEN SON.**

O LORD JESUS-
O SAVIOR WHO HAS COME BACK TO **RESCUE
SINKING US.**

O MIGHTY **KING OF KINGS**-
O DELIVERER OF GOOD AND **HOLY HEAVENLY
THINGS.**

I ADORE YOU, O **LORD FROM ABOVE.**
I WILL ALWAYS TREASURE AND **SHARE YOUR DIVINE
LOVE.**

O MIGHTY GOD AND **DIVINE SAVIOR**-
O HEAVENLY KING OVER YOUR **BLESSED SON AND
DAUGHTER.**

YOU **GIVE US**-
THE DIVINE STRENGTH THAT COMES WITH KNOWING,
RESPECTING, AND FOLLOWING THE WAY THAT
LEADS TO SALVATION THROUGH **THE LIVING GOD,
CHRIST JESUS.**

OH HOLY **REALM OF LOVE-**
WE ARE GRATEFUL FOR THE HELP THAT DESCENDS
FROM **SWEET HEAVEN ABOVE.**

O **HOLY GROUND-**
WE ARE TRULY GRATEFUL THAT YOU ARE **ALWAYS
AROUND.**

HOLY, HOLY, HOLY-
IS THE HELPFUL GOD ALMIGHTY!!!

FOR, YOU, O LORD GOD, **TRULY EXIST-**
AND YOU DO WALK **IN OUR BLESSED MIDST.**

HOLY, HOLY, HOLY-
**IS THE EXISTENCE OF CHRIST JESUS, THE
ALMIGHTY!!!**

AND WHEN I SEARCHED FOR MY HOLY GOD

BARBARA SPEAKING

WHEN I SEARCHED FOR **MY HOLY GOD-**
THE GATES OF SWEET HEAVEN OPENED VERY WIDE,
SO THAT ALL MAY **EXPERIENCE HIS DESCENDED
LOVE.**

MY BLESSED SOUL **SOUGHT HIM DAILY-**

Barbara Ann Mary Mack

YES, I SOUGHT THE AIDE THAT I NEEDED FROM CHRIST **JESUS, THE ALMIGHTY.**

I SOUGHT **HIS DIVINE LOVE-**
THAT DESCENDED WITH HIM FROM **SWEET HEAVEN ABOVE.**

WHEN MY BLESSED SOUL SEARCHED FOR **ALMIGHTY GOD, THE HOLY ONE-**
I FOUND THE HOLY SPIRIT OF GOD, **THE FATHER'S, ONLY BEGOTTEN SON.**

I SEARCHED, AND I **SEARCHED, YOU SEE-**
AND MY SEARCHING SOUL FOUND THE HOLY ESSENCE OF **GOD, THE BLESSED TRINITY.**

I HAVE FOUND HIM! I HAVE FOUND HIM! I HAVE **FOUND HIM, YOU SEE-**
I HAVE FOUND THE HOLY SPIRIT OF ALMIGHTY GOD, **THE FOREVER-EXISTING TRINITY.**

FOR, HIS SPIRIT HAS **ALWAYS, YOU SEE-**
BEEN IN THE PRESENCE OF THE LOVED ONES WHO BELIEVE IN **GOD, THE ALMIGHTY.**

HOLY, HOLY, HOLY-
IS THE BLESSED SPIRIT OF CHRIST JESUS, THE **ALMIGHTY!!!**

YOU HEARD MY CRIES, O LORD

BARBARA SPEAKING TO CHRIST JESUS

YOU HEARD MY CRIES: YOU HEARD MY CRIES. YOU,
O HOLY GOD, ALWAYS HEAR-
MY EVERY FALLEN TEAR.

HOLY, HOLY, HOLY-
IS THE SINGLE FALLEN TEAR THAT I SHARE WITH
MY HEAVENLY GOD ALMIGHTY!!!

YOU HEARD, YOU HEARD, YOU, O HOLY GOD, HEARD
MY HUMBLE CRY.
AND, I AM TRULY GRATEFUL, O LORD GOD, FOR YOU
DID NOT PASS ME BY.

YOU GAVE ME THE DIVINE STRENGTH THAT I WOULD
NEED-
AND, I AM GRATEFUL FOR THE SPIRITUAL
NOURISHMENT THAT YOU DID FEED.

FOR, YOU FED ME YOUR DIVINE STRENGTH, YOU SEE-
THAT I WOULD NEED TO ACCOMPLISH THE
CHALLENGES THAT FACED HUMBLED ME.

OH HOW GRATEFUL-

Barbara Ann Mary Mack

TO BE IN THE HOLY PRESENCE OF THE GOD WHO IS
TRULY **ETERNAL AND WONDERFUL.**

OH HOW **GRAND-**
TO BE PLACED IN YOUR **HELPING HOLY HAND.**

FOR, **HOLY AND TRUE-**
IS THE HAND THAT BELONGS TO THE BLESSED
HELPING YOU.

HOLY, HOLY, HOLY-
IS THE HAND AND LOVE OF CHRIST JESUS, THE
ALMIGHTY!!!

YOU HELPED ME, MY GOD

BARBARA SPEAKING TO ALMIGHTY GOD

YOU, **O HOLY HELPER-**
HELPED ME AND **MY BLESSED DAUGHTER.**

THROUGH HER DIVINE **PERSISTENCE-**
YOU REVEALED **YOUR HOLY PRESENCE.**

THROUGH HER BOLDNESS **AND PERSISTENCE-**
YOU MADE KNOWN **YOUR HOLY PRESENCE.**

WE ARE TRULY **GRATEFUL, MY GOD.**

FOR, YOU CONSTANTLY REVEAL YOUR HOLY
PRESENCE AND LOVE.

HOLY, HOLY, HOLY-
IS THE PRESENCE AND HELP OF GOD ALMIGHTY!!!

FOR, YOUR HOLY PRESENCE AND SPIRIT MOVES,
YOU SEE-
IN THE MIDST OF MY BLESSED CHILDREN AND ME.

HOLY, HOLY, HOLY-
IS THE SPIRITUAL ASSISTANCE OF GOD ALMIGHTY!!!

THE HOLY SPIRIT HAS DESCENDED IN THE MIDST OF
MY DAUGHTER.
SHE TOO, HAS EXPERIENCED THE HOLY PRESENCE
AND HELP FROM GOD, OUR HEAVENLY ETERNAL
FATHER.

LA TOYA TOO, HAS EXPERIENCED OUR GOD'S VISIBLE
PRESENCE-
AND THE REVELATION OF HIS TRUE EXISTENCE.

HOLY, HOLY, HOLY-
IS THE VISIBLE PRESENCE OF JEHOVAH GOD, THE
ALMIGHTY!!!

Barbara Ann Mary Mack

THE REALM OF HOLINESS AND DIVINE GOODNESS
HAS CAPTURED OUR GRATEFUL HEARTS

BARBARA SPEAKING TO THE LORD GOD

O LORD GOD: LET OUR REALM OF GRATITUDE-
JOIN THE PRAISES OF YOUR HEAVENLY MULTITUDE.

FOR, HOLY, YOU SEE-
IS THE GOD WHO HELPED MY BLESSED DAUGHTER
AND ME.

HOLY, HOLY, HOLY-
IS THE HELPFUL AND MERCIFUL GOD ALMIGHTY!!!

HOLY, HOLY, HOLY-
IS GOD, THE FATHER, ALMIGHTY!!!

YOU COMPLETED AND FULFILLED MY DIVINE
REQUESTS, O LORD GOD

BARBARA SPEAKING TO THE LORD GOD

THANK YOU. THANK YOU. THANK YOU, LORD JESUS.
THANK YOU FOR HONORING THE REQUESTS OF THE
FAITHFUL AND THE RIGHTEOUS.

THANK YOU. THANK YOU. THANK YOU-

IT GIVES ME GREAT PLEASURE AND GRATITUDE TO
SERVE THE ONLY LIVING GOD WHO IS HOLY, ETERNAL
AND TRUE

I AM TRULY GRATEFUL-
TO SERVE A GOD WHO IS MERCIFUL, COMPASSIONATE
AND WONDERFUL.

I TRULY-
ADORE AND REVERE GOD ALMIGHTY.

HOLY, HOLY, HOLY-
IS THE REVERENCE THAT I HAVE AND EXHIBIT FOR
GOD ALMIGHTY!!!

HOLY, HOLY, HOLY-
IS THE REVERED CHRIST JESUS, THE ALMIGHTY!!!

IN THE LAND OF NEED

BARBARA SPEAKING

IN THE LAND OF NEED, YOU SEE-
MY BLESSED SPIRIT SEARCHED FOR GOD, THE
ALMIGHTY.

MY SOUL SEARCHES ABOVE THE HEAVENS, DAILY-

Barbara Ann Mary Mack

SEEKING HELP FROM ALMIGHTY GOD; **SWEET ETERNITY.**

HOLY, HOLY, HOLY-
IS THE SOUL THAT SEEKS THE PRESENCE OF SWEET ETERNAL GLORY.

SEEK, SEEK; **SEEK, THE ALMIGHTY!**
SEEK HIM, AS HE GOVERNS **SWEET ETERNITY!**

SEEK, SEEK; SEEK-
BEHOLD THE GOD WHO LOVES AND **GOVERNS THE MEEK.**

FOR, HE **DOES EXIST-**
HE NOW, TRULY, WALKS **IN OUR BLESSED MIDST.**

FOR, **EARTH'S NEEDS-**
TRANSCEND A WORD THAT HAS LIMITS TO ONE THAT **EARTH FEEDS.**

FOR, EARTH'S BARREN **LAND, YOU SEE-**
CANNOT FEED THE CHILDREN WHO **BELONG TO GOD ALMIGHTY.**

HOLY, HOLY, HOLY-
IS THE LAND THAT IS GOVERNED AND RULED BY GOD ALMIGHTY!!!

MY BLESSED SOUL NEEDS **THE LORD JESUS**-
FOR, HE LOVES AND GUIDES THOSE WHO **ARE**
PRECIOUS.

THE LORD **JESUS**-
IS COMMITTED TO THE FAITHFUL ONES **AND THE**
RIGHTEOUS.

FOR, **HOLY AND TRUE**-
IS THE LORD GOD WHO FEEDS ME **AND BLESSED YOU.**

HOLY IS THE LORD GOD **WHO FEEDS**-
THOSE WHO HAVE DIVINE **SEEKING NEEDS.**

HOLY, HOLY, HOLY-
IS THE GOD OF THE NEEDY.

THE NEED FOR A DIVINE **UNINTERRUPTED LOVE**-
THAT DESCENDED FROM **SWEET HEAVEN ABOVE.**

FOR, I HAVE **A NEED**-
FROM THE GOD AND HOLY SPIRIT **AS THEY FEED.**

FOR, I NEED **THAT LOVE**-
TO HELP GUIDE EARTH'S RESIDENTS TO **SWEET**
HEAVEN ABOVE.

I NEED THE **LOVE, YOU SEE**-

Barbara Ann Mary Mack

THAT GUIDES **OBEDIENT ME.**

FOR, **HOLY AND REAL-**
IS THE LOVE THAT I **DESIRE TO FEEL.**

HOLY, HOLY, HOLY-
IS THE NEED FOR CHRIST JESUS, THE LIFE-SAVING
AND REWARDING GOD ALMIGHTY!!!

FOR, HIS HOLY SPIRIT **FULFILLS, YOU SEE-**
ALL OF THE EARTHLY NEEDS OF **MY FAMILY AND ME.**

HOLY, HOLY, HOLY-
IS THE ASSISTANCE THAT I RECEIVE FROM CHRIST
JESUS, THE ETERNAL ALMIGHTY!!!

BOOK # THREE

IN THE PEACEFUL TOMB WITH THE LIVING CHRIST JESUS

IN THE PEACEFUL TOMB WITH THE LIVING CHRIST JESUS

BY:

BARBARA ANN MARY MACK

IN THE PEACEFUL TOMB WITH THE LIVING CHRIST JESUS

SUBTITLE:

I AM WITH YOU, LORD JESUS

BY:

BARBARA ANN MARY MACK

BEGAN: SEPTEMBER 2, 2024

COMPLETED: SEPTEMBER 5, 2024

INTRODUCTION

IN YOUR SWEET TOMB OF VICTORY-
I WILL STAY NEXT TO THE PHYSICAL BODY OF MY
LORD AND GOD ALMIGHTY.

YOU WILL NOT STAY ALONE IN YOUR TOMB OF
VICTORY-
FOR BARBARA, YOUR EARTHLY DAUGHTER, WILL
BE WITH YOU THROUGHOUT SWEET ETERNITY.

I WILL TREASURE AND ADORE YOUR COURAGEOUS
ACT OF DIVINE LOVE-
UNTIL I MEET YOU AGAIN IN SWEET HEAVEN ABOVE.

FOR, HOLY AND TRUE-
IS THE LOVE THAT I HAVE AND SHARE WITH YOU.

FOR, YOU, CHRIST JESUS-
HAVE MADE A GREAT SACRIFICE FOR YOUR
EARTHLY LOVED ONES AND THE RIGHTEOUS.

THERE IS NOTHING THAT WILL KEEP ME AWAY FROM
YOUR TOMB OF LOVE-
FOR, I TRULY DESIRE TO SPEND SWEET ETERNITY
WITH YOU IN HEAVEN ABOVE.

HOLY, HOLY, HOLY-
IS MY VICTORIOUS SAVIOR CALLED CHRIST JESUS,
THE ALMIGHTY!!!

IN YOUR SWEET BLESSED TOMB OF DIVINE LOVE,
DEAR HOLY ONE-
I WILL STAY WITH GOD, THE FATHER'S, ONLY
BEGOTTEN SON.

HOLY, HOLY, HOLY-
IS THE BLESSED TOMB OF CHRIST ALMIGHTY!!!

WITHIN GOD'S PEACEFUL TOMB OF DIVINE LOVE

BARBARA SPEAKING

IN THE TOMB; THE PEACEFUL TOMB, WITH THE
LIVING ETERNAL CHRIST JESUS.
IN THE TOMB, THE PEACEFUL TOMB, WITH THE
FOREVER-LIVING GOD WHO DIED FOR US.

IN THE TOMB, THE GLORIOUS TOMB, WITH THE LIVING
GOD WHO SAVES US.
IN THE TOMB, THE PEACEFUL TOMB, WITH THE
LIVING GOD WHO APPRECIATES THE FAITHFUL ONES
AND THE RIGHTEOUS.

BARBARA SPEAKING TO THE FOREVER-LIVING SPIRIT OF THE CRUCIFIED LORD JESUS

OH, **LOVING JESUS-**
I WILL SIT AT YOUR SIDE IN THE PEACEFUL TOMB OF GOD, **THE FATHER'S, RIGHTEOUS.**

I WILL SIT BY YOUR GLORIOUS AND **VICTORIOUS SIDE-**
AS I BEHOLD AND WITNESS A DIVINE LOVE FOR US THAT **YOU DID NOT HIDE.**

FOR, YOUR LOVE FOR US **IS HOLY AND TRUE-**
IT IS A LOVE THAT SEES **YOUR CHOSEN ONES THROUGH.**

LORD GOD: I WILL SIT BY YOUR WOUNDED AND **PHYSICALLY LIFELESS SIDE-**
FOR, YOU EXHIBITED A DEVOTION TO US THAT YOU **REFUSED TO ABANDON AND HIDE.**

YOUR UNSELFISH DEVOTION-
SAVED MANY OF YOUR WORTHY AND **FAITHFUL CHILDREN.**

MY BLESSED SOUL BOWS IN **YOUR HOLY PRESENCE-**
AS I SIT AT THE HOLY SIDE THAT PROCLAIMS AND VALIDATES **YOUR WELCOMED EXISTENCE.**

FOR, HOLY AND REAL-
IS YOUR SACRIFICIAL ACT OF LOVE THAT I CAN SEE
AND FEEL.

HOLY, HOLY, HOLY-
IS THE SACRIFICIAL ACT OF CHRIST JESUS, THE
ALMIGHTY!!!

LORD JESUS-
YOU HAVE GIVEN UP A LOT FOR THE SINNERS AND
THE RIGHTEOUS.

YOU HAVE TEMPORARILY-
GIVEN UP THE HEAVENLY THRONE OF OUR FATHER'S
ONLY BEGOTTEN SON; CHRIST JESUS, THE ALMIGHTY.

HAVE GIVEN UP YOUR HEAVENLY GLORY-
THAT REVEALS YOUR HOLY LIFE AND DIVINE STORY.

YOU HAVE DESCENDED FROM SWEET HEAVEN-
SO THAT YOU MAY DWELL IN THE MIDST OF YOUR
EARTHLY CHILDREN.

FROM SWEET HEAVEN, YOU CAME DOWN TO US-
SO THAT WE MAY GET A BRIEF GLIMPSE OF THE
FORETOLD MESSIAH CALLED CHRIST JESUS.

Barbara Ann Mary Mack

BARBARA SPEAKING TO THE FOREVER-LIVING SPIRIT OF THE CRUCIFIED LORD JESUS

OH, HOW **GRAND IT IS**-
TO SIT IN THE HOLY ROYAL TOMB OF DIVINE MERCY,
COMPASSION, AND LOVE, **THAT IS HIS.**

HOLY, HOLY, HOLY-
IS THE PHYSICAL TOMB OF THE FOREVER-LIVING
CHRIST ALMIGHTY!!!

BARBARA SPEAKING TO THE FOREVER-LIVING SPIRIT OF THE CRUCIFIED LORD JESUS

FOR, **YOUR VICTORY**-
HAS SET US **SINNERS FREE!!!**

LORD JESUS: YOUR VICTORY AND SACRIFICIAL ACT
ON **YOUR LIVING CROSS OF DIVINE LOVE**-
EXHIBITED A DEVOTION THAT DESCENDED FROM
SWEET HEAVEN ABOVE.

BARBARA SPEAKING

HOLY, HOLY, HOLY-
IS THE LIVING TOMB OF GOD ALMIGHTY!!!

MY BLESSED SPIRIT DID **JOIN, YOU SEE**-

THE LIVING SACRIFICIAL BODY OF CHRIST JESUS,
THE FAITHFUL AND DEVOTED GOD ALMIGHTY.

HOLY, HOLY, HOLY-
IS THE SACRIFICIAL ACT OF LOVE CALLED CHRIST
JESUS, THE ALMIGHTY!!!

HOLY, HOLY, HOLY-
IS THE TOMB OF THE FOREVER-LIVING CHRIST
JESUS; THE ALMIGHTY!!!

**BARBARA SPEAKING TO THE FOREVER-LIVING
SPIRIT OF THE CRUCIFIED LORD JESUS**

LORD JESUS: YOUR HOLY TOMB OF LOVE AND MERCY
WAIT FOR THOSE WHO DESIRE TO ASSIST YOU-
BY BRINGING THE CALLED ONES TO THE HOLY GOD
WHO IS ETERNAL AND TRUE.

BARBARA SPEAKING

FOR, HOLY IS HE-
WHO HAS OBTAINED THE VICTORY.

**BARBARA SPEAKING TO THE FOREVER-LIVING
SPIRIT OF THE CRUCIFIED LORD JESUS**

I WILL CONTINUE TO SIT BY YOUR HOLY SIDE-

AS WE EXHIBIT A DIVINE LOVE THAT YOU AND I
REFUSE TO ABANDON AND HIDE.

BARBARA SPEAKING TO THE FOREVER-LIVING
SPIRIT OF THE CRUCIFIED LORD JESUS

FOR, HOLY, YOU SEE-
IS CHRIST JESUS, OUR LIVING VICTORY.

FOR, HIS SACRIFICIAL ACT OF LOVE EXHIBITED HIS
DIVINE BRAVERY-
AS HE FULFILLED THE PROMISE OF OUR HEAVENLY
GOD AND FATHER ALMIGHTY.

HOLY, HOLY, HOLY-
IS THE VICTORIOUS CHRIST ALMIGHTY!!!

BARBARA SPEAKING TO THE FOREVER-LIVING
SPIRIT OF THE CRUCIFIED LORD JESUS

FOR, YOUR HOLY TOMB OF LOVE-
DESCENDED FROM SWEET HEAVEN ABOVE.

HOLY, HOLY, HOLY-
IS CHRIST JESUS' TOMB OF LOVE THAT WAS CALLED
INTO EXISTENCE BY GOD, THE FATHER, ALMIGHTY!!!

I WILL SIT BY YOUR HOLY SIDE, MY VICTORIOUS GOD, SAVIOR, AND ETERNAL LOVE-
UNTIL YOUR HOLINESS ASCEND TO SWEET HEAVEN ABOVE.

I WILL SIT BY YOUR LOVELY SIDE, AS I WATCH OVER YOUR PRECIOUS WOUNDED LIFELESS PHYSICAL BODY.
AS I GIVE PRAISE, GLORY, AND HONOR, TO OUR HEAVENLY GOD AND FATHER ALMIGHTY.

FOR, HE SAW TO IT-
THAT YOUR PRECIOUS LIFELESS BODY AND I, WERE SURROUNDED BY YOUR HOLY SPIRIT.

SLUMBER, SLUMBER, SLUMBER, O BLESSED SAVIOR.
SLUMBER IN YOUR HOLY TOMB OF LOVE WITH ME, UNTIL YOU REJOIN ALMIGHTY GOD, OUR HEAVEN FATHER.

SLUMBER, SLUMBER, SLUMBER-
IN THE HOLY PRESENCE OF ALMIGHTY GOD, OUR ORIGIN AND MIGHTY FATHER.

FOR, HOLY, YOU SEE-
IS THE GOD AND FATHER WHO WATCHES OVER YOU AND ME.

Barbara Ann Mary Mack

MY LORD: MY HOLY GOD; MY **HEAVEN SENT LOVE.**
I WILL WAIT WITH YOUR WOUNDED AND BRUISED
BODY UNTIL **YOU ASCEND INTO ETERNAL GLORY
ABOVE.**

YOUR HOLY BODY-
IS A VALUE THAT CAME FROM OUR **HEAVENLY GOD
ALMIGHTY.**

FOR, **HOLY AND TRUE-**
IS THE GOD AND FATHER WHO GAVE ROYAL AND
HOLY SACRIFICIAL YOU.

FOR, JEHOVAH GOD, **OUR FATHER, YOU SEE-**
GAVE US HIS **CHRIST JESUS, HIS VICTORY.**

HOLY, HOLY, HOLY-
IS CHRIST JESUS' VICTORY!!!

HOLY, HOLY, HOLY-
IS GOD, THE FATHER'S, ONLY BEGOTTEN SON; HIS
HEAVEN SENT VICTORY!!!

I WILL SIT IN YOUR PEACEFUL **TOMB, LORD JESUS-**
FOR, YOU HAVE GIVEN UP MANY HEAVENLY THINGS;
TO SAVE GRATEFUL US.

HOLY, HOLY, HOLY-

IS THE VICTORIOUS LORD GOD ALMIGHTY!!!

LORD JESUS: I WILL NOT FALL ASLEEP-
FOR, YOUR PRECIOUS WOUNDED AND STILL BODY,
MY GRATEFUL EYES WOULD LIKE TO BEHOLD AND
KEEP.

FOR, HOLY, YOU SEE-
IS THE STILLNESS OF YOUR PHYSICAL LIFELESS
BODY.

HOLY, HOLY, HOLY-
IS THE STILLNESS OF YOUR PHYSICAL LIFELESS
DIVINE ROYAL BODY!!!

I WILL SIT NEXT TO YOUR STILL PHYSICAL LIFELESS
ROYAL BODY-
AS MY SPIRIT UNITES WITH OUR HEAVENLY GOD
AND FATHER ALMIGHTY.

HOLY, HOLY, HOLY-
IS THE PRESENCE OF GOD, OUR FATHER, ALMIGHTY!!!

FOR, I HAVE JOINED, YOU SEE-
THE HOLY PRESENCE OF OUR HEAVENLY GOD AND
FATHER; JEHOVAH, THE ALMIGHTY.

FOR, HE TOO-

SITS IN YOUR EARTHLY TOMB OF LOVE WITH ME AND YOU.

HOLY, HOLY, HOLY-
IS THE PRESENCE OF JEHOVAH GOD, THE HEAVENLY ALMIGHTY!!!

FOR, HE WEEPS, YOU SEE-
WITH FAITHFUL AND DEVOTED ME.

HOLY, HOLY, HOLY-
ARE THE TEARS THAT COME FROM JEHOVAH GOD ALMIGHTY!!!

HOLY, HOLY, HOLY-
ARE MY TEARS THAT HAVE UNITED WITH THE FALLING TEARS OF GOD, THE FATHER, ALMIGHTY!!!

TEACH ME, LORD JESUS

BARBARA SPEAKING TO THE LORD JESUS, AS HE LAYS IN HIS VICTORIOUS TOMB OF DIVINE LOVE

TEACH ME, O LORD JESUS, AS I SIT AT YOUR HOLY ROYAL SIDE.
TEACH ME YOUR VERSION OF DIVINE LOVE THAT YOU DID NOT HIDE.

TEACH ME, LORD GOD, FOR I AM LISTENING.
TEACH ME HOW TO LEAD YOUR EARTHLY LOVED
ONES TO YOUR LAND OF THE LIVING.

FOR, I CAN HEAR YOUR HOLY SPIRIT AS YOU SPEAK
TO ME.
I CAN HEAR THE SILENT WHISPERS OF MY
SACRIFICIAL GOD ALMIGHTY.

LORD JESUS: I AM LISTENING-
TO THE HOLY SPIRIT OF CHRIST JESUS, MY FOREVER-
LIVING GOD AND KING.

I CAN HEAR YOUR HOLY VOICE AS YOU LAY STILL IN
YOUR HOLY TOMB OF DIVINE LOVE.
I CAN HEAR YOUR SWEET HOLY VOICE AS YOU
RECEIVE OUR HEAVENLY FATHER'S BLESSINGS
FROM ABOVE.

I WILL SIT QUIETLY-
AS YOU AND I LISTEN TO THE HOLY VOICE OF OUR
HEAVENLY FATHER ALMIGHTY.

BARBARA SPEAKING

FOR, HOLY, YOU SEE-
IS THE MELODIOUS VOICE OF JEHOVAH GOD, THE
ALMIGHTY.

HOLY, HOLY, HOLY-
IS THE VOICE AND PRESENCE OF OUR HEAVENLY
FATHER; JEHOVAH GOD, THE ALMIGHTY!!!

I WILL WAIT WITH THE FATHER'S ONLY BEGOTTEN
SON OF DIVINE LOVE-
UNTIL HIS BLESSED SPIRIT ENTERS HEAVEN'S HOLY
GATES ABOVE. .

I WILL WAIT PATIENTLY-
WITH THE RISEN CHRIST ALMIGHTY.

FOR, HIS GLORIOUS EXISTENCE-
GIVES JOY TO ALL WHO ACKNOWLEDGE HIS HOLY
PRESENCE.

FOR, HE IS THE VICTORIOUS HOLY ONE-
HE IS GOD, THE FATHER'S, ONLY BEGOTTEN SON.

HOLY IS CHRIST JESUS, THE SACRIFICIAL LAMB OF
DIVINE LOVE-
ETERNAL IS THE FATHER WHO BEGOT HIS HEAVEN
SENT LAMB WITH BLESSINGS FROM SWEET HEAVEN
ABOVE.

HOLY, HOLY, HOLY-
IS THE SACRIFICIAL SON OF GOD, THE FATHER,
ALMIGHTY.

HOLY IS THE **LAMB OF GOD**-
ETERNAL IS HIS SPIRIT OF **DIVINE LOVE.**

I AM SITTING NEXT TO **THE STILL BODY**-
OF MY ETERNAL **GOD ALMIGHTY.**

FOR, MANY YEARS **AGO, YOU SEE**-
HE CALLED INTO EXISTENCE **BLESSED ME.**

HOLY, HOLY, HOLY-
IS MY **CREATOR AND GOD ALMIGHTY!!!**

**BARBARA SPEAKING TO THE LORD JESUS, AS HE
LAYS IN HIS VICTORIOUS TOMB OF DIVINE LOVE**

LORD JESUS: MY BLESSED SPIRIT MOVES IN THE
MIDST OF **YOUR BODY'S STILLNESS**-
AS I CLING TO YOUR GOODNESS, **GREATNESS, AND
HOLINESS.**

HOLY, HOLY, HOLY-
ARE THE GOODNESS AND GREATNESS OF CHRIST
JESUS, THE SACRIFICED GOD ALMIGHTY!!!

MY LORD JESUS: I WILL LAY MY WEARY HEAD UPON
THE STILLNESS OF **YOUR HOLY PRECIOUS BODY**-

Barbara Ann Mary Mack

AS I CLING TO THE COMFORT THAT IS RELEASED
FROM MY LORD AND **GOD; THE ETERNAL CHRIST
ALMIGHTY.**

I WILL LAY MY BLESSED HEAD UPON YOUR **STILL
BEAT-LESS HEART-**
FOR, I KNOW THAT OUR DIVINE UNION **WILL NEVER
PART.**

BARBARA SPEAKING

HOLY, HOLY, HOLY-
IS THE **BEAT-LESS HEART OF MY GOD ALMIGHTY!!!**

HE IS **THE HOLY ROYAL KING-**
THAT WILL **FOREVER REIGN!**

HE IS MY **ETERNAL SOUL MATE-**
WHO HAS THE KEY THAT UNLOCKS SWEET **HEAVEN'S
BEAUTIFUL GATE-**

HOLY, HOLY, HOLY-
IS THE **VICTORIOUS BEAT-LESS HEART OF CHRIST
JESUS, THE ALMIGHTY!!!**

HOLY, HOLY, HOLY-
IS THE **LIFELESS KING ALMIGHTY!!!**

FOR, HE STILL **RULES, YOU SEE-**
IN THE PRIVILEGED PRESENCE OF FAITHFUL AND
WORTHY OBEDIENT ME.

HOLY, HOLY, HOLY-
IS MY VICTORIOUS GOD AND ETERNAL KING; CHRIST
ALMIGHTY!!!

MY BLESSED SPIRIT AND SOUL **BOW, YOU SEE-**
FOR, I AM IN THE HOLY PRESENCE OF THE
SPIRITUALLY LIVING **CHRIST JESUS, THE ALMIGHTY.**

HOLY, HOLY, HOLY-
IS THE STILL BODY OF CHRIST JESUS, THE ETERNAL
GOD ALMIGHTY!!!

MY HUMBLED AND WEARY HEAD WILL **REST,**
YOU SEE-
UPON THE LIFELESS BODY OF CHRIST **JESUS; SWEET**
ETERNITY.

HOLY, HOLY, HOLY-
IS JESUS' LIFELESS BODY!!!

IN OUR SWEET PEACEFUL TOMB, LORD JESUS

BARBARA SPEAKING TO THE HOLY SPIRIT OF THE
FOREVER-LIVING CHRIST JESUS

IN OUR SWEET TOMB OF **DIVINE LOVE-**
OUR UNITED SPIRITS WILL REACH OUT TO GOD, OUR
HEAVENLY FATHER, ABOVE.

OUR UNITED SPIRITS WILL BOW IN THE HOLY
PRESENCE OF **GOD ALMIGHTY-**
AS WE WITNESS HIS HOLY SPIRIT AND **DIVINE
BEAUTY.**

HOLY IS THE PRESENCE OF GOD, THE FATHER'S,
ONLY BEGOTTEN SON.
ETERNAL IS THE FAME THAT **HIS VICTORY HAS WON.**

REST, REST. REST WITHIN YOUR **TOMB OF DIVINE
BEAUTY.**
REST IN THE HOLY PRESENCE OF **OUR HOLY GOD
ALMIGHTY.**

FOR, **HIS TEARS-**
HAVE SHED FOR US **THROUGH THE YEARS.**

HOLY, HOLY, HOLY-
**ARE THE MANY TEARS OF GOD, OUR FATHER,
ALMIGHTY!!!**

FOR, HE AND I **DO WEEP-**
AS MY SAVIOR, CHRIST **JESUS, DOES SLEEP.**

SLEEP WITHIN YOUR TOMB OF **SWEET DIVINITY AND LOVE-**
SLEEP, LORD JESUS, UNTIL OUR HEAVENLY FATHER CALLS YOU **BACK HOME ABOVE.**

FOR, **HOLY AND TRUE-**
IS THE LOVE THAT I HAVE FOR **SACRIFICIAL YOU.**

HOLY IS THE SWEET TOMB THAT GAVE BIRTH TO **OUR LORD JESUS-**
SWEET HEAVEN IS THE PLACE WHICH GOD, OUR FATHER, SPOKE THE HOLY WORDS THAT RELEASED THE TOMB OF LOVE FOR HIS ONLY BEGOTTEN SON; **THE HEAVEN DESCENDED RIGHTEOUS.**

BEHOLD CHRIST JESUS, THE RIGHTEOUS ONE.

LOOK UPON OUR SAVIOR, AS HE LIE STILL AFTER COMPLETING THE DIVINE ASSIGNMENT OF THE FATHER'S ONLY BEGOTTEN SON.

FOR, ONLY CHRIST JESUS-
COULD PAY THE VERY HIGH PRICE FOR SINFUL US.

HOLY, HOLY, HOLY-
IS THE VICARIOUS ACT OF CHRIST ALMIGHTY!!!

FOR, HE TOOK THE PLACE, YOU SEE-

Barbara Ann Mary Mack

OF THE SINFUL CHILDREN OF **GOD ALMIGHTY.**

**HOLY, HOLY, HOLY-
WAS THE VICARIOUS ACT OF CHRIST JESUS, THE
ALMIGHTY!!!**

HIS SACRIFICIAL ACT OF **DIVINE LOVE-**
COMPLETED THE ASSIGNMENT THAT CAME FROM
OUR HEAVENLY **GOD AND FATHER ABOVE.**

**HOLY, HOLY, HOLY-
WAS THE VICARIOUS ACT OF CHRIST JESUS; GOD,
THE ALMIGHTY!!!**

FOR, HE TOOK THE PLACE OF US SINFUL ONES, BY
DYING FOR US ON **HIS CROSS OF DIVINE LOVE.**

**HOLY, HOLY, HOLY-
IS THE VICARIOUS ACT OF CHRIST JESUS, THE
SACRIFICIAL LAMB OF GOD ALMIGHTY!!!**

**HOLY, HOLY, HOLY-
IS THE HEAVEN SENT TOMB OF CHRIST JESUS, THE
ALMIGHTY!!!**

FOR, HE NOW **RESTS, YOU SEE-**

WITHIN THE TOMB THAT WAS APPROVED AND SANCTIFIED BY OUR HEAVENLY GOD AND FATHER ALMIGHTY.

HOLY, HOLY, HOLY-
ARE THE TEARS AND ASSIGNMENT OF GOD, THE FATHER, ALMIGHTY!!!

LORD JESUS: I WILL SIT BY YOUR VICARIOUS SIDE AS YOU LAY VERY STILL IN YOUR DIVINE TOMB OF LOVE. FOR YOU HAVE TAKEN THE PLACE OF US SINNERS. WE, THE BELIEVING ONES, TRULY APPRECIATE YOUR DIVINE ACT OF SACRIFICIAL LOVE

BARBARA SPEAKING TO THE LORD JESUS, AS SHE JOINS HIM IN HIS SACRED TOMB OF LOVE

MY HOLY GOD AND SAVIOR-
YOUR STILL LIFELESS PHYSICAL BODY COMFORTS ME, YOUR WEEPING DAUGHTER.

I WILL SIT BY YOUR HOLY SIDE VERY QUIETLY-
AS I HOLD ON TO THE SWEET VICTORIOUS MEMORIES OF MY GOD AND SAVIOR; CHRIST ALMIGHTY.

I WILL SIT VERY STILL-
AS I CARRY OUT THE FATHER'S HOLY WILL.

FOR, **HOLY AND TRUE**-
IS MY EVERLASTING LOVE FOR **HOLY, ROYAL YOU.**

I WILL SIT VERY STILL, BY YOUR HOLY SIDE, **MY LORD JESUS-**
I WILL SIT BY THE HOLY SIDE OF **HE WHO HAS SAVED US.**

FOR, YOU ARE **THE LIVING VICTORY**-
WHO WAS SENT TO US BY OUR HEAVENLY **GOD AND FATHER ALMIGHTY.**

<u>**BARBARA SPEAKING**</u>

FOR, HE, ALMIGHTY GOD, THE FATHER, OFFERED **HIS ONLY BEGOTTEN SON**-
AS A SACRIFICE **FOR EVERYONE.**

HOLY, HOLY, HOLY-
IS THE SACRIFICIAL ACT OF LOVE CALLED CHRIST JESUS, THE LORD AND GOD ALMIGHTY!!!

HOLY AND TRUE-
IS THE LORD GOD AND SAVIOR WHO DIED ON HIS CROSS OF LOVE **FOR BLESSED ME AND YOU.**

OUR LORD JESUS' HOLY TOMB OF LOVE HAS CALLED ME

OUR LORD JESUS' HOLY TOMB HAS **CALLED
BLESSED ME-**
TO STAY NEXT TO THE STILL LIFELESS **BODY OF**
CHRIST ALMIGHTY.

HIS HOLY TOMB **CALLS OUT, YOU SEE-**
TO FAITHFUL AND **OBEDIENT ME.**

FOR, GOD, THE FATHER, AND I, WILL NEVER LEAVE
HIS PRECIOUS **ONLY BEGOTTEN SON ALONE.**
FOR, NOW, HE IS SITTING UPON HIS MIGHTY **ROYAL**
AND DIVINE THRONE.

HOLY, HOLY, HOLY-
IS THE LIVING THRONE OF CHRIST JESUS, THE
VICTORIOUS GOD ALMIGHTY!!!
YOUR TOMB, MY TOMB; OUR TOMB OF DIVINE LOVE

BARBARA SPEAKING TO THE CRUCIFIED LORD
JESUS IN HIS DIVINE TOMB OF LOVE

MY LORD JESUS: YOUR HOLY TOMB **IS THE**
SANCTUARY-
FOR FAITHFUL AND **TRUSTING ME.**

YOUR TOMB OF **DIVINE LOVE-**

HAS DESCENDED TO YOU AND I **FROM SWEET HEAVEN ABOVE.**

FOR, ALMIGHTY GOD, **OUR HEAVENLY FATHER-** HAS APPROVED OF THE TOMB THAT TEMPORARILY ENCOMPASSES HIS ONLY BEGOTTEN SON, AND BARBARA, **HIS ROYAL OBEDIENT DAUGHTER.**

BEING- IN THE HOLY PRESENCE OF CHRIST JESUS, THE SACRIFICIAL ROYAL KING, IS AN **EVERLASTING GREAT TRIUMPHANT THING.**

BEING- IN THE HOLY TOMB OF DIVINE LOVE WITH THE VICTORIOUS **ROYAL GOD AND KING-** IS AN AWESOME ONCE IN A CHOSEN LIFETIME **EXPERIENCE AND THING.**

BEING IN THE HOLY TOMB OF DIVINE LOVE WITH CHRIST JESUS, THE ROYAL KING, IS **AN AWESOME LIFETIME EXPERIENCE-** THAT IS ORCHESTRATED AND APPROVED BY **GOD, THE FATHER'S, HOLY PRESENCE.**

FOR, **HOLY, YOU SEE-**

IS THE ROYAL PRESENCE OF JEHOVAH GOD ALMIGHTY.

IN CHRIST JESUS' DIVINE TOMB OF LOVE I WILL WAIT

BARBARA SPEAKING

IN THE DIVINE TOMB OF LOVE I WILL WAIT AND SEE-
THE SPIRIT AND BODY OF THE RISEN CHRIST JESUS,
THE ALMIGHTY.

FOR, HOLY, YOU SEE-
IS THE FORETOLD PASSAGE AND PROPHECY OF THE RISEN CHRIST ALMIGHTY.

I WILL WAIT. I WILL WAIT. I WILL WAIT-
FOR CHRIST JESUS' HOLY PRESENCE TO ENTER HEAVEN'S OPEN GATE.

FOR, HOLY, YOU SEE-
IS THE GOD WHO WAITS PATIENTLY WITH BLESSED ME.

HOLY, HOLY, HOLY-
IS THE RISEN GOD ALMIGHTY!!!

WITHIN THE ROYAL TOMB OF DIVINE LOVE

BARBARA SPEAKING THE SPIRIT OF THE CRUCIFIED LORD JESUS IN HIS TOMB OF DIVINE LOVE

WITHIN THE ROYAL TOMB OF DIVINE LOVE, I WILL WAIT FOR YOU TO RISE, **MY LORD GOD.**
FOR, YOU AND I WAIT FOR GOD, THE FATHER'S, **WORDS OF DIVINE LOVE.**

FOR. HIS HOLY **WORDS, YOU SEE-**
WILL IGNITE THE HOLY SPIRIT THAT LIVES IN THE MIDST OF **CHRIST JESUS AND BLESSED ME.**

WE WILL WAIT FOR GOD, THE FATHER'S, **HOLY WORDS OF LOVE-**
TO SUMMON CHRIST JESUS' ASCENSION **INTO SWEET HEAVEN ABOVE.**

FOR, **HOLY, YOU SEE-**
ARE THE HEAVEN SENT WORDS THAT WILL IGNITE THE BEING OF **CHRIST JESUS, THE ALMIGHTY.**

FOR, AS HE **LAY STILL-**
HE CONTINUES TO DO **THE FATHER'S HOLY WILL.**

HOLY, HOLY, HOLY-
IS THE OBEDIENCE OF THE CRUCIFIED CHRIST **ALMIGHTY!!!**

FOR, HIS WOUNDED AND LIFELESS ROYAL BODY, YOU SEE-
WILL NOT RISE AGAIN, UNTIL THE FATHER COMMANDS THE HOLY WORDS THAT WILL IGNITE CHRIST JESUS' BELOVED BODY.

HOLY, HOLY, HOLY-
IS CHRIST JESUS' WOUNDED LIFELESS BODY!!!

HIS HOLY TOMB OF LOVE IS CALLING YOU AND ME

BARBARA SPEAKING TO GOD'S EARTHLY CHOSEN FEW

DEAR CHILDREN:
YES! MY BROTHERS AND SISTERS FROM EVERY EARTHLY NATION.

CHRIST JESUS' HOLY TOMB IS CALLING YOU AND ME-
KING JESUS' TOMB OF DIVINE LOVE IS CALLING THOSE WHO ARE CHOSEN BY CHRIST, THE ALMIGHTY.

IT IS CALLING, YOU SEE-
YOU AND BLESSED ME.

FOR, HOLY AND TRUE-
IS THE TOMB OF DIVINE ROYAL LOVE THAT CALLS BLESSED ME AND YOU.

HOLY, HOLY, HOLY—
IS THE LIVING TOMB OF CHRIST JESUS, THE
ALMIGHTY!!!

FOR, HIS ASCENSION INTO **SWEET HEAVEN**—
WILL REVEAL HIS LOVE FOR ME AND **HIS GREATEST
CREATION.**

HOLY, HOLY, HOLY—
IS THE FORETOLD ASCENSION OF CHRIST JESUS, THE
ALMIGHTY!!!

FOR, HE **WAITS, YOU SEE**—
FOR THE FATHER'S WORDS THAT WILL **SET HIS
LOVED FREE.**

HOLY, HOLY, HOLY—
IS THE FORETOLD ASCENSION OF GOD ALMIGHTY!!!

HOLY, HOLY, HOLY—
IS THE STILL LIFELESS BODY OF THE ROYAL CHRIST
JESUS, THE ALMIGHTY!!!

IT IS TIME FOR YOU TO RISEAGAIN, LORD JESUS

BARBARA SPEAKING TO THE CRUCIFIED LORD
JESUS IN HIS EARTHLY TOMB OF DIVINE LOVE

IT IS TIME FOR YOU TO **RISE, LORD JESUS.**
IT IS TIME FOR YOU TO PROCLAIM YOUR VICTORY
OVER **SIN AND THE UNRIGHTEOUS.**

IT IS TIME FOR THE **WHOLE WORLD TO SEE-**
THE HOLY PRESENCE OF **THE RISEN GOD ALMIGHTY.**

FOR, **HOLY AND TRUE-**
IS THE ASCENSION THAT IS **CALLING OBEDIENT YOU.**

HOLY, HOLY, HOLY-
IS CHRIST JESUS' ASCENSION INTO HEAVENLY
GLORY!!!

FOR, CHRIST **JESUS, YOU SEE-**
IS GOD, THE FATHER'S, ONLY BEGOTTEN **SON; THE
ALMIGHTY**

MY SPIRITUAL MIND, BODY AND SOUL BOW, AS I SIT
IN THE DIVINE TOMB OF THE CRUCIFIED LORD JESUS;
MY SAVIOR AND GOD

BARBARA SPEAKING

MY SPIRITUAL MIND, BODY AND SOUL BOW, AS I **WAIT
PATIENTLY-**
IN THE BLESSED SANCTIFIED TOMB OF CHRIST
JESUS, THE VICTORIOUS GOD ALMIGHTY.

I WAIT PATIENTLY-
FOR THE HOLY WORDS OF GOD, OUR FATHER, TO
SUMMON THE STILL **LIFELESS BODY OF CHRIST, THE
ALMIGHTY.**

FOR, THE HOLY WORDS OF **GOD, THE FATHER-**
WILL GIVE LIFE TO THE STILL LIFELESS BODY OF
THE ONLY BEGOTTEN SON, **AS THE RIGHTEOUS ONES
GATHER.**

HOLY, HOLY, HOLY-
IS THE STILL LIFELESS BODY OF CHRIST JESUS, THE
FOREVER-LIVING GOD ALMIGHTY!!!

HOLY, HOLY, HOLY-
IS THE STILL PEACEFUL BODY OF CHRIST JESUS,
THE HEAVEN SENT ALMIGHTY.

HOLY, HOLY, HOLY-
IS THE WAITING CHRIST ALMIGHTY!!!

AND NOW, I WILL RISE, SAYS THE LORD JESUS

THE RISEN LORD JESUS SPEAKING

I WILL RISE, **SAYS THE LORD JESUS-**

MY WOUNDED BODY OF DIVINE LOVE WILL RISE
IN THE PRESENCE OF **GOD, MY FATHER, AND THE
RIGHTEOUS.**

I WILL **RISE, YOU SEE-**
I WILL RISE IN THE HOLY PRESENCE OF **GOD, THE
FATHER, ALMIGHTY.**

FOR, **HOLY, YOU SEE-**
IS THE POWER OF THE RISEN GOD AND SAVIOR; THE
FOREVER-LIVING CHRIST JESUS, THE ALMIGHTY.

I WILL RISE! I WILL RISE! **I WILL RISE, YOU SEE-**
IN THE PRESENCE OF THOSE WHO WERE **CHOSEN BY
GOD ALMIGHTY.**

I WILL **RISE, YOU SEE-**
IN THE MIDST OF GOD, THE **FATHER'S, SWEET
REALITY.**

I WILL **RISE, YOU SEE-**
IN THE HOLY PRESENCE OF **HEAVEN'S GLORY.**

FOR, **HOLY AND REAL-**
IS MY RISEN PRESENCE THAT THE CHOSEN ONES
WILL **SURELY SEE AND FEEL.**

HOLY, HOLY, HOLY-

IS THE VICTORIOUS CHRIST JESUS' WOUNDED RISEN BODY!!!

HOLY, HOLY, HOLY-
IS CHRIST JESUS, THE RISEN KING OF VICTORY!!!

IN YOUR HOLY TOMB OF DIVINE LOVE, I WILL DWELL, MY GOD

BARBARA SPEAKING TO THE LORD JESUS IN HIS TOMB OF DIVINE LOVE

IN YOUR HOLY **TOMB OF DIVINE LOVE-**
I WILL **DWELL, MY GOD.**

I WILL PONDER OVER **YOUR HOLY STORY-**
UNTIL YOU RISE TO **ETERNAL GLORY.**

I WILL WAIT WITH YOU **PATIENTLY-**
AS YOU BRING SWEET CLOSER TO YOUR HOLY **HEAVEN ORDERED STORY.**

I WILL WATCH AND WAIT UNTIL **I BEHOLD AND SEE-**
YOU FULFILL THE HOLY ASSIGNMENT THAT WAS GIVEN TO YOU BY **OUR HEAVENLY FATHER AND GOD ALMIGHTY.**

FOR, **HOLY AND TRUE-**

IS THE GOD AND FATHER WHO SENT HOLY AND
OBEDIENT YOU.

RISE! RISE! RISE, O BLESSED SAVIOR ON MINE!

**BARBARA SPEAKING TO THE CRUCIFIED LORD
JESUS IN HIS TOMB OF DIVINE LOVE**

RISE, O BLESSED SAVIOR AND GOD OF MINE!
RISE FROM YOUR BLESSED TOMB OF DIVINE LOVE
DURING THIS NEEDY TIME.

RISE, IN THE HOLY PRESENCE OF JEHOVAH GOD, THE
ALMIGHTY.
RISE, O BLESSED ONE, SO THAT ALL MAY BELIEVE
AND SEE!

MAKE KNOWN YOUR HOLY RESURRECTION, SO THAT
ALL MAY BEHOLD AND SEE-
THE DIVINE BEAUTY OF THE RISEN CHRIST
ALMIGHTY.

RISE. RISE. RISE, O BELOVED RISEN ONE!
RISE, O VICTORIOUS ONLY BEGOTTEN SON!!!

FOR, YOU HAVE COMPLETED AND FULFILLED YOUR
FORETOLD DIVINE ASSIGNMENT OF DIVINE LOVE-

Barbara Ann Mary Mack

THAT WAS GIVEN TO YOU FROM **GOD, OUR HEAVENLY FATHER, ABOVE.**

HOLY, HOLY, HOLY-
IS THE FULFILLED ASSIGNMENT OF GODLY LOVE BY CHRIST JESUS, THE ALMIGHTY!!!

HOLY, HOLY, HOLY-
IS THE VICTORY OF THE RISEN CHRIST ALMIGHTY!!!

FOR, HIS DEVOTION AND **LOVE, YOU SEE-**
HAVE PIERCED THE MIND AND HEART THAT **BELONG TO BLESSED ME.**

HOLY, HOLY, HOLY-
IS THE RISEN CHRIST JESUS, THE ALMIGHTY!!!

FOR, HE RULES AND **REIGNS, YOU SEE-**
IN THE MIDST OF HIS BLESSED EARTHLY **LOVED ONES AND ME.**

I WILL BATHE IN THE MIDST OF **HIS GLORY-**
AS I PROCLAIM THE REALITY OF HIS **HOLY RISEN STORY.**

HOLY, HOLY, HOLY-
IS THE BLESSED GOD, THE ALMIGHTY!!!

THE RISEN CHRIST JESUS

BARBARA SPEAKING

THE RISEN CHRIST JESUS-
HAS PROCLAIMED VICTORY IN THE MIDST AND
PRESENCE OF THE FAITHFUL ONES AND THE
RIGHTEOUS.

HOLY, HOLY, HOLY-
ARE THE RIGHTEOUS LOVED ONES WHO ARE
FAITHFUL TO THE RISEN ETERNAL GOD ALMIGHTY!!!

FOR, HIS HOLY SPIRIT AND PRESENCE MOVES,
YOU SEE-
IN THE MIDST OF THE EARTHLY BLESSED ONES
AND ME.

BEHOLD, O EARTHLY LANDS

BARBARA SPEAKING

BEHOLD, O EARTHLY BLESSED LANDS!
BEHOLD THE GLORY AND POWER OF THE LIVING AND
RISEN CHRIST JESUS' HOLY HANDS!

LOOK UPON HIS RISEN GLORY-
AS I PROCLAIM HIS SPECTACULAR HOLY STORY.

Barbara Ann Mary Mack

FOR, MY BLESSED EYES, YOU SEE-
DID BEHOLD THE FULLNESS OF THE RISEN GOD
ALMIGHTY!!!

HOLY, HOLY, HOLY-
IS THE ASCENDED CHRIST ALMIGHTY!!!

FOR, I HAVE WITNESSED, YOU SEE-
THE MARVELOUS ASCENSION OF GOD ALMIGHTY.

I DID BEHOLD-
HIS ASCENSION INTO THE LAND THAT IS MORE
VALUABLE THAT EVERY PHYSICAL AND SPIRITUAL
POT OF GOLD.

I REALLY DID SEE

BARBARA SPEAKING

I SAW IT! I SAW IT! I REALLY SAW IT!
I SAW IT, BY THE POWER OF ALMIGHTY GOD'S HOLY
SPIRIT!

I DID! I DID! I REALLY DID SEE-
THE RISEN LORD JESUS ASCEND INTO HEAVENLY
GLORY.

FOR, IT WASN'T A DREAM, AND IT WASN'T A
FANTASY-
I REALLY SAW OUR LORD JESUS ASCEND INTO
SWEET HEAVENLY GLORY.

I DID NOT RUN, AND, I DID NOT HIDE-
FOR, MY BLESSED SPIRIT WAS STILL BY HIS
VICTORIOUS SIDE.

FOR, HOLY, YOU SEE-
WAS THE VISION OF SWEET DIVINE ECSTASY.

HOLY, HOLY, HOLY-
IS THE SWEET REALITY OF THE RISEN CHRIST
ALMIGHTY!!!

FOR, HE NOW REIGNS, YOU SEE-
IN THE MIDST OF HEAVENLY GLORY.

HOLY, HOLY, HOLY-
IS THE ASCENDED CHRIST JESUS; THE RISEN GOD
ALMIGHTY!!!

RISE! RISE! RISE, O BLESSED SAVIOR!!!

BARBARA SPEAKING TO THE RISEN CHRIST JESUS

RISE! RISE! RISE, O BLESSED SAVIOR!

RISE IN THE HOLY PRESENCE OF JEHOVAH GOD, **OUR HEAVENLY ORIGIN AND FATHER.**

RISE! RISE! RISE, ABOVE EVERY **BUILDING'S STORY-** RISE, SO THAT YOU MAY **ENTER HEAVEN'S SWEET GLORY!**

RISE IN THE PRESENCE OF **GOD'S HOLY ANGELS AND GRACE-** RISE, SO THAT YOU MAY TAKE **YOUR HEAVENLY PLACE.**

FOR, YOUR HOLY THRONE WAITS FOR THE PRESENCE OF **YOUR GLORIOUS LIVING FACE-** AS YOU LEAD YOUR **VICTORIOUS HEAVENLY RACE.**

RISE, FOR YOU **ARE NOT ALONE.** RISE, O VICTORIOUS JESUS; AND TAKE YOUR PLACE ON **YOUR MIGHTY HEAVENLY THRONE!**

FOR, **HOLY, YOU SEE-** IS THE HEAVENLY THRONE THAT **WAITS FOR THEE.**

BEHOLD YOUR HEAVENLY PLACE, O RISEN LORD JESUS

<u>BARBARA SPEAKING</u>

BEHOLD. BEHOLD. BEHOLD YOUR HEAVENLY PLACE ON HIGH, **O RISEN VICTORIOUS LORD JESUS!**
BEHOLD THE MIGHTY THRONE THAT **AWAITS THE RIGHTEOUS!**

BEHOLD YOUR RETURN TO **HEAVENLY GLORY!**
BEHOLD THE PRESENCE OF **YOUR HOLY UNENDING STORY!**

RISE, O BLESSED ONE!
TAKE YOUR PLACE ON YOUR MIGHTY THRONE, O BLESSED **ONLY BEGOTTEN SON!**

FOR, YOU NOW, HOLD THE TITLE OF **THE FATHER'S VICTORIOUS SON.**
YOU, O KING OF VICTORY, ARE **THE ETERNAL GLORIOUS ONE!!!**

HOLY, HOLY, HOLY-
IS THE VICTORIOUS CHRIST ALMIGHTY!!!

FOR, GOD, OUR FATHER, **ADORES BLESSED YOU-**
FOR, YOU, O LORD JESUS, DID SEE YOUR **DIVINE ASSIGNMENT THROUGH.**

HOLY, HOLY, HOLY-
IS THE RISEN VICTORIOUS CHRIST ALMIGHTY!!!

I WILL RISE, DEAR BARBARA, SAYS THE CRUCIFIED LORD JESUS

THE CRUCIFIED LORD JESUS, SPEAKING TO BARBARA, HIS SENT MESSENGER

I WILL RISE, **DEAR BARBARA.**
I WILL ASCEND INTO ETERNAL GLORY IN THE BLESSED PRESENCE OF **MY DEVOTED AND FAITHFUL DAUGHTER.**

FOR, YOU DESERVE **TO BEHOLD-**
THE DIVINE ASCENSION THAT IS MORE VALUABLE THAN EVERY POT OF **EARTHLY AND HEAVENLY GOLD.**

VICTORIOUS SAVIOR ALMIGHTY: THE RISEN LORD JESUS

BARBARA SPEAKING

MY VICTORIOUS **SAVIOR ALMIGHTY-**
YOU ARE VERY VALUABLE **AND PRECIOUS TO ME.**

MY VICTORIOUS SAVIOR ALMIGHTY, NOW REIGNS, YOU SEE-
IN THE MIDST OF HIS EARTHLY LOVED ONES AND ME.

HOLY, HOLY, HOLY-
IS THE ROYAL RISEN CHRIST ALMIGHTY!!!

FOR, HIS **VICTORY OVER SATAN-**
BRINGS SALVATION TO PEOPLE **FROM EVERY NATION.**

HOLY, HOLY, HOLY-
IS THE RISEN CHRIST ALMIGHTY!!!

FOR, HIS VICTORY OVER **DEATH, YOU SEE-**
REVEALS THE LOVE AND DEVOTION THAT **HE HAS**
FOR YOU AND ME.

HOLY, HOLY, HOLY-
IS THE DEVOTION AND FAITHFULNESS OF GOD
ALMIGHTY!!!

HOLINESS; CHRIST JESUS, HAS ASCENDED INTO
HEAVENLY GLORY

BARBARA SPEAKING TO EARTH'S RESIDENTS
TODAY

HOLINESS; CHRIST JESUS, HAS ASCENDED **INTO**
HEAVENLY GLORY-
AND NOW, WE MAY CONTINUE LEARNING OF HIS
HOLY **GOD ORCHESTRATED STORY.**

HE NOW, **DOES RESIDE-**
BY OUR HEAVENLY GOD AND **FATHER'S, HOLY SIDE.**

OH, **HOW GRAND-**
TO WITNESS THE HOLY PRESENCE OF THE VICTORIOUS
CHRIST JESUS, AS HE **FULFILLED THE FATHER'S
VICTORIOUS PLAN.**

FOR, **HOLY AND TRUE-**
IS THE CHRIST WHO SUFFERED FOR **ME AND
BLESSED YOU.**

HOLY, HOLY, HOLY-
IS THE VICTORIOUS RISEN CHRIST ALMIGHTY!!!

FOR, **HIS VICTORY-**
HAS **SET US FREE-**

FREE FROM SIN AND **EVERLASTING DESTRUCTION.**
FOR, WE ARE GOD'S **WORTHY AND FAITHFUL
CHILDREN.**

CHRIST JESUS-
IS THE **VICTORY WHO SAVES US.**

HOLY, HOLY, HOLY-
IS OUR RISEN LORD AND GOD ALMIGHTY!!!

THE GLORY OF THE RISEN LORD JESUS SHINES

BARBARA SPEAKING

THE GLORY OF THE LORD SHINES, AS THE VICTORIOUS CHRIST JESUS ENTERS HEAVEN'S SWEET OPEN GATES AGAIN. FOR, HIS GLORY-
REVEALS HIS GOD ORDERED DIVINITY.

FOR, GOD, OUR HEAVENLY FATHER, YOU SEE-
HAS GIVEN HIS ONLY BEGOTTEN SON FULL POSITION AS THE VICTORIOUS AND FAITHFUL CHRIST ALMIGHTY.

FOR, HE IS THE DIVINE ROYAL ONE.
HE IS THE FATHER'S ONLY BEGOTTEN OBEDIENT SON.

HE IS THE FAITHFUL ONE, YOU SEE-
FOR, HE CARRIES OUT EVERY ASSIGNMENT THAT COMES FROM GOD, THE FATHER, ALMIGHTY.

HOLY, HOLY, HOLY-
IS THE OBEDIENT CHRIST ALMIGHTY!!!

IMITATE ME, SAYS THE RISEN VICTORIOUS CHRIST JESUS

THE RISEN VICTORIOUS CHRIST JESUS SPEAKING

Barbara Ann Mary Mack

IMITATE ME, MY EARTHLY **SON AND DAUGHTER.**
IMITATE HE WHO IS OBEDIENT TO THE DIVINE
ASSIGNMENTS THAT ARE GIVEN TO US BY THE
GREAT AND ALMIGHTY **GOD AND FATHER.**

IMITATE ME-
IMITATE THE BLESSED AND **BELOVED TRINITY.**

FOR, **WE ARE ONE-**
IN UNION WITH THE **FATHER AND THE SON.**

IN UNION WITH **GOD, THE HOLY SPIRIT-**
WHO WHISPERS, AND **THE BLESSED ONES HEAR IT.**

HOLY, HOLY, HOLY-
IS THE INSEPARABLE UNION WITH GOD, THE FATHER,
ALMIGHTY!!!

FOR, HE, THE FATHER ALMIGHTY, CALLS INTO
EXISTENCE, YOU SEE-
EVERYTHING THAT PLEASES THE GREAT AND
POWERFUL ALMIGHTY.

HOLY, HOLY, HOLY-
IS GOD, THE BLESSED AND **WELL-LOVED TRINITY!!!**

BEHOLD. BEHOLD. BEHOLD. LOOK UPON THE RISEN KING, WHO IS MORE VALUABLE THAN STREAMS AND STREAMS OF PURE FINE GOLD.

BARBARA SPEAKING

BEHOLD THE RISEN ROYAL KING-
AS HIS SUBJECTS AND I JOIN THE HEAVENLY CHOIRS AS THEY SWAY AND SING.

LIFT UP YOUR HEAVENLY VOICES, O GREAT AND HOLY MULTITUDE-
AS THE HEAVENLY HOSTS AND I RELEASE OUR DEVOTION AND GRATITUDE.

FOR, THE MIGHTY KING, YOU SEE-
BOWS IN THE HOLY PRESENCE OF GOD, THE FATHER, ALMIGHTY.

LIFT US YOUR UNIFIED VOICE-
AS YOUR BLESSED SPIRITS REJOICE!!!

FOR, CHRIST, THE RISEN VICTORIOUS KING, YOU SEE-
BOWS IN THE HOLY PRESENCE OF GOD, THE FATHER AND ME.

HOLY, HOLY, HOLY-
IS THE VICTORIOUS RISEN CHRIST ALMIGHTY!!!

Barbara Ann Mary Mack

AND HE, THE VICTORIOUS KING JESUS, SAT ON HIS MIGHTY THRONE ON HIGH

<u>**BARBARA SPEAKING**</u>

AND, THE VICTORIOUS KING JESUS, SAT ON HIS MIGHTY THRONE IN THE MIDST OF HIS HOLY ANGELS AND HEAVEN'S GREAT MULTITUDE; **THE SANCTIFIED SAINTS.**
WHERE, THERE ARE NO **RESTRICTIONS NOR RESTRAINTS.**

FOR, OUR BLESSED **SPIRITS, YOU SEE-**
FLY FREE IN THE DIVINE PRESENCE **OF GOD ALMIGHTY.**

HE SAT **DOWN, YOU SEE-**
ON HIS MIGHTY THRONE ON HIGH, **NEXT TO ME.**

OH, WHAT A GRAND AND **GLORIOUS SIGHT-**
TO WITNESS CHRIST JESUS' **VICTORY AND HOLY MIGHT.**

OH, HOW **GRAND IT IS-**
TO HAVE A HOLY THRONE ON HIGH, **RIGHT NEXT TO HIS.**

HOLY, HOLY, HOLY-

IS THE GLORY AND THRONE OF CHRIST JESUS, THE ALMIGHTY!!!

OH, HOW GRAND-
TO BE A PART OF HIS HOLY LAND.

FOR, HOLY AND TRUE-
IS THE HEAVENLY KING WHO RESCUES BLESSED YOU.

HOLY, HOLY, HOLY-
IS THE REVERENCE OF GOD ALMIGHTY!!!

FOR, HE RULES, YOU SEE-
IN THE MIDST OF SWEET INFINITY.

HOLY, HOLY, HOLY-
IS THE VICTORY OF GOD ALMIGHTY!!!

AND I BEHELD THE VISIBLE PRESENCE OF THE GREAT AND HOLY RISEN ONE

BARBARA SPEAKING

YES: I BEHELD THE VISIBLE PRESENCE OF CHRIST JESUS, THE GREAT AND HOLY RISEN ONE!
MY BLESSED EYES AND SOUL BEHELD THE LIVING BEING OF CHRIST JESUS; GOD, THE FATHER'S, ONLY BEGOTTEN SON.

I BEHELD HIS HOLY PRESENCE IN THE MIDST OF **HIS HEAVENLY GLORY.**
I BEHELD THE RISEN ONE, AS HE CONFIRMED HIS RESURRECTION AND **HIS HOLY STORY.**

FOR, HIS **RESURRECTION, YOU SEE-**
REVEALS HIS DEATH AND LIFE BEFORE AND AFTER HE WAS CONDEMNED AND **NAILED TO THE CROSS FOR YOU AND ME.**

HOLY, HOLY, HOLY-
IS THE CRUCIFIXION AND RESURRECTION OF CHRIST ALMIGHTY!!!

FOR, HIS PHYSICAL DEATH AND RESURRECTION **RULES, YOU SEE-**
IN THE BLESSED PRESENCE OF **YOU AND ME.**

HOLY, HOLY, HOLY-
ARE THE DEATH AND RESURRECTION OF THE FOREVER-LIVING CHRIST ALMIGHTY!!

FOR, HIS HOLY SPIRIT AND PRESENCE **MOVE, YOU SEE-**
IN THE MIDST OF **YOU AND ME.**

HOLY, HOLY, HOLY-
ARE THE SPIRIT AND PRESENCE OF CHRIST JESUS, THE ALMIGHTY!!!

I DID **BEHOLD, YOU SEE**-
THE GREAT PRESENCE OF THE DIVINE KING WHO
SAT ON HIS HOLY THRONE **NEXT TO WORTHY ME.**

HOLY, HOLY, HOLY-
IS THE THRONE OF GOD ALMIGHTY!!!

FOR, HE RULES AND **REIGNS, YOU SEE**-
FROM HIS MIGHTY THRONE THAT **SITS NEXT TO ME.**

HAIL, HAIL, HAIL, TO **THE MIGHTY KING ON HIGH**-
HAIL TO HIS MIGHTY THRONE THAT SITS ABOVE THE
WORLD'S BRIGHT BLUE SKY!

HAIL TO CHRIST JESUS; THE FOREVER-LIVING RISEN
KING OF DIVINE PEACE!
HAIL TO THE HOLY ONE WHOSE HOLY WORDS **HE DID**
RELEASE!
HAIL! HAIL! HAIL, TO THE **GREAT KING ALMIGHTY!**
HAIL AND PRAISES TO THE GOD WHO HAS DIED ON
HIS CROSS OF DIVINE LOVE FOR **EVERY EARTHLY**
BODY!!!

GLORY TO GOD **IN THE HIGHEST**-
GLORY AND HOLY TO THE RISEN KING, FOR HE IS
ABOUT TO REVEAL HIS GREATNESS.

Barbara Ann Mary Mack

GLORY TO THE HIGHEST KING WHO IS ABOUT TO
CONTINUE WITH THE UNVEILING OF **HIS HOLY UNTOLD
STORY!!!**

HAIL, O MIGHTY KING **OF ENDLESS GLORY-**
HAIL TO CHRIST JESUS' **HOLY UNENDING STORY!!!**

FOR, IT IS **REVEALED, YOU SEE-**
THAT CHRIST JESUS IS THE GREAT AND HOLY
UNCHANGING GOD ALMIGHTY!!!

HOLY, HOLY, HOLY-
IS THE UNCHANGING GOD ALMIGHTY!!!

AND, YOU AND I WILL GO DOWN TO EARTH, DEAR
BARBARA

THE RISEN LORD GOD SPEAKING TO BARBARA

YOU AND I WILL GO DOWN **TO EARTH, DEAR
BARBARA.**
WE WILL VISIT THE CHILDREN OF **ALMIGHTY GOD,
YOU FATHER!**

WE WILL GO **DOWN TO SEE-**
THE TROUBLED CHILDREN THAT **BELONG TO ME.**

BARBARA SPEAKING TO HEAVEN'S INHABITANTS

BOW. BOW. BOW, O BLESSED HEAVENLY CREATION!
BOW IN THE HOLY PRESENCE OF THE RISEN LORD
JESUS, YOU BLESSED NATION!

FOR, HOLY IS THE GLORIOUS RISEN KING-
ETERNAL IS HIS MIGHTY REIGN!!!

FOR, HE DOES REIGN, YOU SEE-
IN THE PRESENCE OF HIS SWEET VICTORY.

MIGHTY IS THE RESURRECTED KING-
ETERNAL IS HIS HOLY REIGN!

HOLY, HOLY, HOLY-
IS THE ROYAL GOD ALMIGHTY!!!

WITNESS HIS PEACEFUL GLORY-
AS HE PREPARES FOR HIS HOLY STORY.

AND WHEN CHRIST JESUS, THE FOREVER-LIVING
DIVINE ROYAL KING, ROSE FROM HIS HEAVENLY
THRONE.

BARBARA SPEAKING

WHEN CHRIST JESUS, THE FOREVER-LIVING GOD AND
KING ROSE FROM HIS MIGHTY THRONE THE GREAT
MULTITUDE AND I BOWED IN HIS HOLY PRESENCE.

Barbara Ann Mary Mack

FOR, THE HOLY KING AND I, WERE NOW IN OUR PERMANENT HEAVENLY RESIDENCE.

HOLY, HOLY, HOLY-
IS THE PERMANENT RESIDENCE OF GOD ALMIGHTY AND ME.

I WILL RISE FROM MY HEAVENLY THRONE, YOU SEE-
AND MOVE FREELY WITHIN THE HOME THAT WAS PREPARED FOR THE EARTHLY RIGHTEOUS ONES AND ME.

HOLY, HOLY, HOLY-
IS THE HEAVENLY HOME THAT WAS PREPARED FOR US BY GOD, THE FATHER, ALMIGHTY!!!

AS I MOVE WITHIN-
I AM GREETED BY CHRIST JESUS, MY HEAVENLY FRIEND.

FOR, THE BLESSED HOLY TRINITY-
AS ONE UNITED ENTITY-
GREETS AND WELCOMES WORTHY SANCTIFIED ME.

HOLY, HOLY, HOLY-
IS CHRIST JESUS, MY HEAVENLY GOD AND FRIEND;
THE ALMIGHTY!!!

FOR, THE BLESSED HOLY TRINITY, YOU SEE-
IS THE FAITHFUL FRIEND WHO WELCOMES
GRATEFUL ME.

HOLY, HOLY, HOLY-
IS MY ETERNAL FRIEND; THE BELOVED TRINITY!!!

OH, WHAT A GRAND AND GLORIOUS EXPERIENCE,
YOU SEE-
TO DWELL IN THE MIDST OF GOD'S HEAVENLY
RESIDENCE WITH THE BLESSED TRINITY.

OH, SUCH A DELIGHTFUL EXPERIENCE-
TO BE A PART OF GOD'S HOLY RESIDENCE.

HOLY, HOLY, HOLY-
IS GOD'S HEAVENLY RESIDENCE AND THE HOME OF
THE BLESSED TRINITY!!!

MY BLESSED INVITED SPIRIT MOVES, YOU SEE-
WITHIN THE BELOVED HOME OF GOD ALMIGHTY.

AS MY BLESSED SPIRIT MOVES THROUGHOUT SWEET
HEAVEN

BARBARA SPEAKING

Barbara Ann Mary Mack

AS MY BLESSED SPIRIT MOVES THROUGHOUT THE
MIGHTY **GATES OF SWEET HEAVEN-**
I CAN SEE AND HEAR THE MELODIOUS UNIFIED VOICE
OF **GOD'S CHOSEN CHILDREN.**

I CAN HEAR THE **JOYFUL LAUGHTER-**
AS THEY COMMUNE AROUND **GOD, THE FATHER.**

OH, WHAT A DIVINE **JOY AND DELIGHT-**
TO DWELL WITHIN **THE FATHER'S HOLY SIGHT.**

FOR, HOLY AND **TRUE, YOU SEE-**
IS THE HEAVENLY HOME THAT WELCOMES **THE
BLESSED ONES AND ME.**

HOLY, HOLY, HOLY-
ARE THE CHOSEN GUESTS OF GOD ALMIGHTY!!!

FOR, IT IS **THE HEAVENLY LAND-**
THAT FEELS SAFE AND SECURE WITHIN **GOD, THE
FATHER'S, HOLY HAND.**

HALLELUJAH! HALLELUJAH!
THE LORD JESUS HAS TAKEN HIS RIGHTFUL PLACE
AT HIS MIGHTY THRONE NEXT TO **ALMIGHTY GOD,
THE FATHER, JEHOVAH.**

LET US PRAISE! LET US PRAISE!

LET US PRAISE ALMIGHTY GOD, THE FATHER, GOD, THE VICTORIOUS SON; AND GOD, THE HOLY SPIRIT, THROUGH **THESE PRAISE WORTHY DAYS!!!**

LET THE HEAVENLY CURTAIN **RISE, YOU SEE**-FOR, WE, THE SAVED AND BLESSED ONES, ARE IN THE HOLY PRESENCE OF **ALMIGHTY GOD, THE BLESSED TRINITY!!!**

BARBARA AND BEAUTIFUL BLESSED JUDY, ONE OF GOD'S LITTLE HELPERS ON EARTH TODAY

BARBARA AND ONE OF GOD'S LITTLE ANGELS ON EARTH

BILLY AND HIS BROTHER ANDREW: TWO OF GOD'S HANDSOME SONS

BARBARA AND BEAUTIFUL LISA, ONE OF GOD'S LOVELY DAUGHTERS

HAPPY BIRTHDAY BABY JESUS- 2024

BARBARA NEWSPAPER ONE

149

SOME OF MY OTHER GOD INSPIRED PUBLISHED BOOKS

1. WORDS OF INSPIRATION
2. FATHER, ARE YOU CALLING ME? (CHILDREN'S BOOK)
3. DAUGHTER OF COURAGE
4. A HOUSE DIVIDED CANNOT STAND
5. TASTE AND SEE THE GOODNESS OF THE LORD
6. HUMILITY- THE COST OF DISCIPLESHIP
7. WILL YOU BE MY BRIDE FIRST?
8. ODE TO MY BELOVED
9. FATHER, THEY KNOW NOT WHAT THEY DO
10. IN MY FATHER'S HOUSE (CHILDREN'S BOOK)
11. IN MY GARDEN (CHILDREN'S BOOK)
12. THE BATTLE IS OVER
13. THE GOSPEL ACCORDING TO THE LAMB'S BRIDE
14. THE PRESENT TESTAMENT
15. THE PRESENT TESTAMENT VOL. 2
16. THE PRESENT TESTAMENT VOL. 3
17. THE PRESENT TESTAMENT VOL. 4
18. THE PRESENT TESTAMENT VOL. 5
19. THE PRESENT TESTAMENT VOL. 6
20. THE PRESENT TESTAMENT VOL. 7

Printed in the United States
by Baker & Taylor Publisher Services